CELEBRATE THE HARVESTS!

Celebrate the Harvests!

Michigan Farm Markets, Farm Stands,
and Harvest Festivals

DON *and* NELLE FRISCH

Nelle Frisch
Don Frisch

WILLIAM B. EERDMANS PUBLISHING COMPANY
GRAND RAPIDS, MICHIGAN

To the farm families of Michigan

© 1995 Wm. B. Eerdmans Publishing Co.
255 Jefferson Ave. S.E., Grand Rapids, Michigan 49503
All rights reserved

Printed in the United States of America

00 99 98 97 96 95   7 6 5 4 3 2 1

Library of Congress Cataloging-in-Publication Data

Frisch, Don, 1933-
    Celebrate the harvests! : Michigan farm markets and farm stands /
Don and Nelle Frisch.
        p.   cm.
    Includes bibliographical references
    ISBN 0-8028-7056-2 (paper)
    1. Farm produce — Michigan — Marketing. 2. Farmers' markets —
Michigan. I. Frisch, Nelle, 1924-   . II. Title.
HD9007.M5F75   1995
381'.41'09774 — dc20   95-5
                                                    CIP

Contents

Acknowledgments

WE THANK SAM EERDMANS, WHO ENCOURAGED US TO write this book, believed from the beginning that we could do it, and treated us to lunches as he prodded us to finish. We thank Mary Hietbrink for her kind and gentle editing, and even for what she calls her nitpicking. And we thank the other professionals at Eerdmans who labored to produce this work and, like Mary, improved it in the process.

We thank Brian Lackey and Tish Hendricks at CPI One-Hour Photo Finish, who helped turn our snapshots into photographs.

We thank all the generous people who shared their secrets of produce selection, preparation, and the recipes we've included.

Finally, we thank our out-of-state, grown-up children, who no longer dread the asparagus season, willingly eat zucchini, and now take us to visit their local farm markets.

Authors' Note, or Why We Like Farm Markets

SOME TWENTY YEARS AGO, WHEN WE MOVED FROM CHI-cago to Grand Rapids, we bought a house in the suburbs. It was set aslant on the lot, providing us separate patches of sunlit yard for gardens.

That first winter, we buried ourselves in seed catalogs. Choosing what to plant wasn't easy, but we made a logical decision not to try growing our own corn. We'd plant tomatoes, we thought, zucchini, and some pumpkins. Maybe some peas and lettuce and radishes too.

In early spring we dug up the yard — kind of a sticky, wet soil that clumped on the shovels. On St. Patrick's Day we planted the peas. A couple of weeks later we sowed the lettuce and radish seeds.

Frost killed the young pea plants. The lettuce plants — Grand Rapids lettuce, which should be perfect for our area — reached a height of two inches, then rotted. After the second planting, they grew to three inches before the patch burned out. The radishes flourished above ground, producing huge bunches of leaves. But that sticky soil turned out to be mostly impenetrable builder's clay. The radishes below ground reached the size of small peas, then herniated. We were told that radish leaves are good in salads, but we didn't try that. Instead, we went to the Fulton Street Farmers' Market in Grand Rapids and bought bunches of perfect radishes and heads of Grand Rapids leaf lettuce, plants with normal leaves, each one big enough to fully cover a standard salad plate.

Zucchini, pumpkins (the kids wanted to grow their own jack-o'-lanterns), and tomatoes were to be the heart of our crop. But the tomato dragons attacked and chewed through all the stems while the tomatoes were still small green marbles on the vine. Replanting with vigorous plants from a farm market, we harvested our first bright red, perfect tomato — just when local farmers were selling bushels of equally perfect tomatoes for less than we had paid for our plants.

We watched our zucchini blossoms wither and fall from the vine. Perhaps out of sympathy, anonymous neighbors took to abandoning huge zucchini warclubs on our doorstep in the dead of night. We did harvest a four-inch pumpkin.

Each of our failures we dismissed as a onetime event, and each spring we continued to plant our garden. It took three years for this fact to register with us: farmers — and neighbors — were better at growing vegetables than we were, and our home garden should be reserved for other things.

We had planned to use some of our yard for a cutting garden. But bouquets at the Fulton Street market, starting with tulips and pussy willows in the spring, were so inexpensive that there never seemed a need to cut our own. So the perennial flowers we planted bloom, look pretty against the house, fade, and finally are cut back. Still, our house is always filled with prize specimens, purchased at farm markets or farm stands.

Patient and friendly farmers smiled when we recounted our backyard adventures. It wasn't frost that killed our peas, they told us. Peas survive that trauma. But those farmers laughed out loud when we told them of our St. Pat's Day planting date. Their suggestion: to plant only when the ground is ready. That is sound, if vague, advice, but one old farmer did tell Jim Watson, a friend of ours, the real, professional secret to assure proper spring timing. "Well, on a nice sunny morning, you just go out to the field and wiggle your bare bottom on the earth. When it feels right, a little warm and not too damp, plant the peas." Please note that this procedure should be followed taking considerable care for the sensibilities of proper neighbors.

When we finally quit, admitting freely that professionals

grow better vegetables and flowers than we do, it was all right. By that time we had discovered our farm market, and we've become addicted to it.

Saturday morning at the Fulton Street Farmers' Market has become the time and place for us to see old friends and neighbors. We go to do our shopping, but we spend as much time chatting, admiring kids, and trading recipes. Everybody smiles, yells greetings, and talks. Strangers will come up and say, "Where did you get the raspberries and the baby's breath?" And we preen at their recognition of our cleverness.

We're good at market shopping because we've developed a routine of going to the market early, taking a strong basket, and walking the entire length before buying anything. We're embarrassed, though, to pass a stand without buying something.

That's because we've grown to know the farmers so well that over the years they have almost become family. We've watched their kids grow, become adults, and often leave. They've seen the same happen with ours. So we ask about their families and they ask about ours, while we all proudly stand, sharing pictures of new grandchildren.

The farmers know each other well too, and while they compete for the shoppers' traffic, it is a friendly competition, with people in neighboring stalls helping each other. There's a great deal of mutual respect. Pauline Strick serves as the prime example. When she talks about the other farmers, she always says "Mr. Visser" or "Mrs. Van." Her approach is charming and reflects the dignity of life at the market.

It's not always sweetness and light, however. We weren't there, and we suppose it wouldn't have happened in front of customers, but a number of farmers gleefully remember the day when one farmer grew so angry with a neighbor that he threw a pail of water at her. We never learned what the dispute was about, but farmers were happy to fill us in on the details.

The farmers are more likely to tease each other, particularly during slow times. John Geukes has been the victim of veggie fights with Betty Nitz, his neighbor across the aisle. Toward the end of the day, when customers are scarce, he need only turn his back to be hit by a flying piece of leftover produce. He's not so innocent, and he'll respond in kind.

The farmers at the Fulton Street market are a stable group, and that's part of the reason they relate to each other so well. Jeff Dykstra, a seller at the market as well as its manager, has been coming for fifteen years, and he's a relative newcomer. Leona Van Koevering started coming with her parents, "as a baby," and has been coming for twenty-five years with her husband. Betty Nitz has put in over thirty-five years at the market, and Diane Platt has been coming "as long as the market has been open."

All the farmers work hard to entice shoppers, and they have fun doing it. They'll build produce displays that are a kind of folk art, but better than the usual crafts because you can smell, touch, and taste the art works as well as see them. As you stroll past the stalls, your eye will be caught by a spiral stack of radishes, with the bright red-and-white globes pointing out, sitting next to scarlet beefsteak tomatoes, set in spokes radiating from a cut specimen displayed on an overturned basket. Hand-lettered signs, sometimes adorned with a smiley face or a big "YUMMY," give the prices. To prove that the quality is fine, the farmers often offer tastes, making it even more difficult for shoppers to pass by without buying something.

The lush displays and free tastes don't stop shoppers from asking "Are these the best?" or "Are these ripe?" But these are good questions that the farmers love to answer. If you want a melon for the next day, they'll tell you which one to buy. And they'll be right. If you want to know how to cook the "first picking" beans, they'll suggest a simple, straightforward method. These farmers seldom have time to prepare fancy dishes, and their fruits and vegetables do taste fine without many fixings.

There is an intrinsic honesty to the whole process. We watched two young girls, ten or eleven years old, helping their parents, busily sorting tomatoes into firsts and seconds. When asked about the difference, one responded, "If you slice them, the seconds look just like firsts." The other responded, "Firsts do look better, and that's important."

Farmers also learn from the shoppers. One day, Farmer Ham of the Ham Family Farm had brought in a load of leeks. When a shopper asked him how to use them, he said that his wife put leeks in soups, then added, "A man was just here who said he puts vermouth in his leek soup." Farmer Ham said he would definitely be trying that recipe.

With all this goodwill, and with all this good produce, we, like other shoppers, have difficulty limiting what we buy. So, like everybody else, we'll go to the market for a couple of tomatoes, and then buy berries, peaches, a melon, beans, some colorful peppers, new potatoes, green onions, and a bouquet. We'll truck it all to the car, and then remember to run back and buy the tomatoes we came to get, but forgot.

Consequently, we've been forced to develop a "rational" approach to the excess purchases we make at our farm market: we've taken up freezing, canning, and pickling. Thus, the farm market has provided us with a new and creative hobby that yields a harvest of tasteful memories to last the winter.

Our addiction is worse than you might think. Even when we travel, we'll stop at any farm stand we pass to "pick up some fruit for the hotel room." That's not so bad, but sometimes those stands come up along the road with little notice, so we squeal to a stop, often having to back up to the entrance. The public needs to be warned about people like us, and this note serves that purpose.

A Word about the Recipes

WHILE THIS IS NOT A COOKBOOK, WE'VE INCLUDED SOME recipes to suggest uses for the fine farm products of Michigan. While we make no pretensions to being great or particularly innovative cooks, some of these recipes are old family favorites of ours. We do like to cook, and we do like to eat, as evidenced by the fact that neither of us seems to lose weight easily.

Where did our recipes come from, if we are not inventive? Most were inspired by cookbooks (one of us — Nelle — collects them), but all have become ours through a kind of evolutionary change. For example, we probably started making our poultry stuffing by following the directions on the bread stuffing package, but now we're more fat conscious. So we substitute applesauce for oil and omit or reduce the number of egg yolks. A friend may suggest that we add an herb or two, and so we modify the mix again. We also watch our sodium intake, so we no longer add any salt. We remember childhood, and add some chestnut meats, as one of our mothers (Don's) once did. Finally, we stop consulting the package and just throw the stuffing together. It's ours.

The farmers we talked to thought of "ours" a little differently. When we asked for a recipe, we often got a photocopy of one from a standard American cookbook. We've seen recipes from *Good Housekeeping, Fannie Farmer,* and *Betty Crocker.* And they're all good, the farmers swear by them, and they're readily available to you.

At one food festival we attended, a nice, elderly woman had entered a dish in the food sampling contest. It was a remarkably pretty presentation and tasted great, though it had not won a prize.

We asked her for her recipe, and she gladly showed us an issue of *Gourmet*. She had copied the recipe completely, down to the plate, and was entering it in national as well as local competitions. She certainly didn't think she was stealing somebody's idea or creation. She had made the dish and believed, therefore, that it was her recipe. And that's a common feeling held by farm cooks. If you make it, it's yours.

We've also asked chefs for recipes for dishes we've enjoyed at their restaurants. One published professional chef, when we asked permission to use a recipe, said, "Oh, just change something and call it yours." But we haven't done that. And we haven't tested all the recipes we've included.

It would be almost insulting to test those from professionals who have been kind enough to contribute recipes. They're better cooks than we are, and if they say this is the way to prepare a dish, we'll accept that. Besides, give a recipe to any two people to prepare, and you'll have two different dishes.

We haven't tested the recipes we've included from friends, either, but we've eaten them. (And they've eaten our recipes as well.)

Most of the recipes we've included can be modified to suit the fresh produce available, and many of the recipes can be drastically changed with no ill effect. We include a marinara sauce which for years we told friends came from Dom DeLuise's fine, funny cookbook called *Eat This*. When we went to check the recipe for inclusion in this book, we discovered that his recipe and ours aren't the same at all. Nor do we necessarily make it the same way each time we prepare it.

If you start with fresh Michigan plum tomatoes and add good, strong onions and fresh basil, you'll make good marinara sauce. And if you have a heavy hand with garlic or pepper the day you make it, it doesn't matter. If you run out of time or patience and don't drain the chopped tomatoes long enough, your sauce will be thinner than another time you prepare it. That doesn't matter, either. Other than making it too salty, there's not much you can do to ruin freshly prepared marinara sauce.

So innovate and improvise when you try the recipes we've included. You'll enjoy the process of discovery.

On the Farm

IN THE CUISINE OF THE NINETIES, THE TREND IS TO USE healthier, low-fat foods, so the produce farmer has become king. Supermarkets display cartoon caricatures of hayseeds in straw hats, and one Michigan chain even calls itself "Farmer Jack's." Other chains devote thousands of square feet to year-round displays of fruits and vegetables, including exotic varieties from

This is the kind of farm stand that makes roadside shopping a pleasure.

around the world. Independent grocers and produce stores do the same. For city folks, though, it's refreshing entertainment to take a drive in the country, see the farms, and meet some of the farmers. And if you do, you'll get a better feel for Michigan's produce and what's available from season to season. (Keep in mind that many stands are closed on Sundays. Be sure to call ahead to find out what hours they're open.)

You don't have to travel far. Every city has small farms on its periphery, now often farmed by back-to-the-soil people in love with the romance of growing their own food. Take, for example, Steve Karr and his wife, Melanie, who operate Angela's Garden at 2276 Dean Lake Road N.E., on the fringe of Grand Rapids. Steve doesn't grow enough to quit his day job, and his farm is too small to do anything commercially but "specialize in gourmet herbs and produce." Nonetheless, he's put up a stand for direct sales to drive-by customers.

Angela's Garden

Steve puts it into perspective: "The stand itself is as basic as you probably will see. It is constructed from a shipping pallet, propped up on cement blocks. While most of my product is sold directly to chefs and produce stores, the stand provides two primary benefits. First, there is the satisfaction of providing good, organic produce to my neighbors. Secondly, although the stand hardly produces profit, it does provide sport. To me, operating the stand is much like fishing. In the morning, I select the bait (what items, how much, etc.), throw out the net (open the stand for the day), and then return at dusk to discover what is the day's catch."

That's the spirit of many of the small farmers selling directly to the public. Bigger farmers actually may depend on farm-stand sales for their survival. Signs on the freeways will direct you to the exit to take to find some of these larger farm stands and orchards.

To find several great farm stands as well as other attractions, take M-89 through Fennville. As you drive along I-196 and U.S. 31 (they run together in southwestern Michigan), the exit sign for M-89 tells you that a winery tour is available year-round at Fenn Valley. There you can taste the wines produced from Fenn Valley's grape harvest and walk through their vineyards to see the varieties of growing grapes. Their tasting room has a balcony overlooking the cellar and the aging tanks, and labels explain the

Fenn Valley Winery

wine-making process. Fenn Valley also makes grape juice and nonalcoholic wines (wines from which almost all the alcohol has been removed by cold filtration), a nice alternative for children and those who don't drink. After tasting, you can buy wine by the glass or by the bottle and buy some cheese, then sit for a time on their pleasant deck overlooking the vineyards and just relax.

Conifer Lane Farm

Conifer Lane Farm, close to the exit for Fenn Valley, offers "u-pick" fruit through most seasons. The family provides the bags, boxes, and ladders, and you get the chance to find that perfect peach while it's still on the tree. If picking your own isn't what you want to do, they also sell fruit they've picked, as well as vegetables from their farm and "farm-fresh whole hog" sausages in their "Dutch Apple Barn."

During apple harvest, the owners offer wagon rides to and through the orchard as part of the family entertainment. And throughout the fall, they operate a cider mill, inviting visitors to watch them make fresh cider.

Mann Farms

Mann Farms is another u-pick orchard on M-89, and there you can also pick berries in season. John Mann tells us his raspberries have "only little, itty-bitty stickers."

Al Meeusen — his wife, Leslie, calls him "Farmer Al" — operates a classic farm stand on M-89. He's primarily a peach farmer, growing twelve varieties, but he also sells apples, sweet corn, sweet and hot peppers, tomatoes, basil, cantaloupes, and watermelons, all grown on his farm, Sunrise Orchards. He's par-

Sunrise Orchards

ticularly proud of his 17,000 gladiolas, originally planted to attract customers for his peaches. So his stand is pretty in the summertime, and when fall comes Al decorates it with mounds of pumpkins, bales of hay, and a fine-looking scarecrow.

Al is a professional farmer, with a master's in agriculture from Michigan State University (he often wears a green MSU shirt). He's articulate, and he loves to talk with shoppers about farming. For example, he told us that "1992 was the year of the green tomato," simply too cool for many to ripen. "It was the year it snowed in Alpena on the first day of summer, but it was also the year I was able to pick sweet corn for market in October. It was a strange year," said Al.

He went on to reflect about the ten record-setting warm years that preceded 1992, and then about his family's past experiences

Al Meeusen of Sunrise Orchards.
He enjoys decorating his farm stand for customers.

in Michigan farming, dating back to his "grandmother's great-grandfather," who was drafted from Michigan for service in the Civil War. You'll find that this kind of conversation with farmers adds to the entertainment value of visiting farm stands while it improves your appreciation of the fruits and vegetables you buy.

Crane Orchards   Crane Orchards is a neighboring Centennial farm on M-89 (Al Meeusen actually bought his frontage from the Cranes so that he could have a farm stand). The Cranes sell their apples and other fruits in a big, barn-like building that also houses their "Pie Pantry" restaurant and bakery. They specialize in fresh fruit pies, and a slice of their apple pie topped with a melting dip of rich vanilla ice cream is pure, all-American heaven. The Cranes also operate a bed and breakfast, so you can enjoy a night in a real farmhouse.

Take advantage of that opportunity in mid-October and spend some time at Fennville's Goose Festival. A refuge south of Fennville, the Todd Farm, is a stopover spot for 300,000 migratory geese. The town (and hunters) celebrate the yearly arrival of the geese with a parade on M-89 in the center of town, a pancake breakfast, a sidewalk sale, a craft show, popcorn wagons, food sales (yes, you can get cooked goose), and hunting.

There are a number of other farm stands on or near M-89 in Fennville, but M-89 is by no means unique in providing an entertaining country experience. Even busy highways close to the heart of metropolitan centers in Michigan afford this kind of fun. Take the East Beltline of Grand Rapids as another example. Sietsema Orchards is a large fruit grower with a vineyard that abuts the Beltline and a cider mill just east of the Beltline on Three Mile Road. The Sietsemas run a classic fruit stand/cider mill operation, with fresh-picked fruit on sale from a wagon parked next to the Beltline, and more fruit on sale at the mill. In the fall they have pumpkins, grapes, apples by the bag and by the bushel, caramel apples, apple pies, doughnuts and cider, and even apple wood for home fireplaces. In the main shop during harvest time, all you hear is the rumble of apples rolling down a conveyor belt to the cider mill, and laughter from customers and staff having a rollicking good time.

Sietsema Orchards

Robinette's Orchards, located on the Beltline with the entrance on Four Mile Road, operates a cider mill, a bakery, and a snack bar. In addition, the Robinettes have turned one building into a "gift barn," filled with country-style decorations and limited-issue collectibles. Jim Robinette, the apple farmer, is an articulate, well-informed, entertaining man who's fun to chat with. He delights in pointing out the details on the imported ceramic miniature houses he sells and will regale you with stories about the artists. In fact, he's willing to talk about everything from his merchandise to golf to politics. But don't expect more than a pleasant hello or advice about apples from Jim during his hectic cider-mill season.

Robinette's Orchards

Mary Bethel Robinette fills the traditional role of the farm wife in a nontraditional manner. She bustles about, supervising the snack bar and the sale of baked goods, sometimes stopping to clear a table, tease an irresistible young visitor, or chat with a friend.

On the weekends during the fall harvest, swarms of customers descend on Robinette's, lining up to buy everything from cider and cider shakes to doughnuts and apples to eat on the lawn. And the Robinettes have extended their season into the winter by serving hot cider and renting equipment for cross-country skiing; ski buffs can use their orchards and an adjacent park.

So Robinette's is busy much of the year, primarily because the farm is fun to visit. And fun is the primary ingredient in all the successful small-farm diversifications we've seen.

Flowers of the Field

Flowers of the Field, on the Beltline between Three and Four Mile Roads, is an example of a family-run farm operation pros-

Robinette's is a great place to go in the fall for cider squeezed-while-you-watch and doughnuts warm from the oven.

pering through diversification and finding a unique niche in the market. The family's dried flowers and herbs became so popular that they built a striking contemporary showroom in which to display them, along with gourds, pumpkins, Indian corn, and decorative grasses, all of which they grow on their farm on Four Mile Road. It's a pleasant, fragrant place, decorated and filled with clever, artful ways to use dried flowers and with well-chosen country accessories — from baskets to pottery to glassware — that are part of their diversification. You'll find that Martin Andre and his parents, Norma and John, make it fun to shop here, welcoming customers by name as they come through the front door. And if you're not a recognized friend already, it won't be long before you become one.

Other cities yield other finds. Like Flowers of the Field, Bluff Gardens in Harbor Springs has built a new showroom and has diversified into sales of decorative housewares and accessories. The owners have become dealers in French faience, an earthenware product covered with opaque glazes and painted with colorful decorations. They started as a distributor of Quimper products, which feature whimsical figures, floral patterns, and birds in the Breton tradition. Now they've expanded to include other lines, one of which includes their own exclusive pattern, Trillium, hand-painted by artists from the Atelier de' Segries, Moustievs, France.

Bluff Gardens

As a farm, Bluff Gardens specializes in fully mature miniature vegetables, to be eaten raw as crudités. And you can't help but smile, or giggle, when you buy a mature patty-pan squash that's not big enough to cover the palm of your hand. Bluff Gardens' season is the summer, when fashionable hostesses on Michigan's gold coast can't seem to have a party without serving pea-sized tomatoes and whole carrots and zucchini no longer than your finger. Often, the hostess will accompany these veggies with an assortment of Bluff Gardens dips and serve them in one of the whimsical, handcut earthenware baskets that can be purchased in the showroom. And while Bluff Gardens now publishes an extensive mail-order catalog of their varied products, it is clearly more fun to visit and see for yourself.

Pat Bourdo and her artist/sculptor husband, Jon, own and operate Woodland Herb Farm outside of Northport on M-22 in the Leelanau Peninsula. They've made their fifteen-acre farm into one of the prettiest sites in Michigan, surrounding their showroom with manicured beds of herbs tailored and arranged by size, color, and fragrance. It's worth a stop just to look and sniff.

The Country Mill

The Country Mill in Charlotte makes no bones about the fact that fun is part of what it sells. The owners' advertising brochure offers "Family Fun on the Farm . . . Fall 'til Christmas." This u-pick apple farm has an "Orchard Express," a tractor-train fixed up to resemble an old-time western locomotive and cars, which takes you to and through the orchards. The owners are clearly train-oriented: after Thanksgiving they open a loft featuring an extensive Lionel Train layout, with the train operating on weekends up to the Sunday before Christmas. Nearby is a fully furnished dollhouse replica of their 150-year-old farmhouse.

In September they run a petting zoo in cooperation with the Eaton County 4-H Youth. In September and October they have sing-alongs in the Old Mill Cider Bar and demonstrations of how to make apple butter and how to use their apple peeler and pie-making machine. In late October they offer a scarecrow contest and a pumpkin carry-off contest. In the carry-off contest, participants (who pay a small fee that may vary from year to year) can keep all the pumpkins they can carry across the finish line. One very large man set the record in 1992, carrying 63 pumpkins at one time. In addition, before Halloween the "Orchard Express" offers a trip down a "haunted trail," where there are Fred and Barney characters to delight little children.

When there's no special event, you can sit in the Old Mill Cider Bar and sip an apple-cider float or shake, or have a simple soup-and-bread meal. Apple pies are a specialty, and you can get a slice in the Cider Bar, or buy a whole pie fresh or frozen to eat at home. They offer half a dozen variations.

Farmer Friday's Market

Farmer Friday's Market in Coloma is another example of a farmer selling fun and entertainment in a diversified operation. Paul Friday — he actually signs his name Paul "Farmer" Friday — started his direct-selling operation as a produce store that offered mostly his own fruit and vegetables. That grew to be a large food store handling cheese, packaged groceries, and wines. He even added a small meat market when he recognized that the expansion of the large chain stores into his area meant he had to find a special niche.

Pat and Jon Bourdo's beautifully landscaped
herb gardens are worth the trip.

Farmer Friday's most enjoyable season was pumpkin time,
when he went all out to make the season fun for the kids. Then,
in 1989, to make Halloween a year-round specialty, he added
hundreds of masks and costumes to his inventory and opened
his "Halloween Center of America." "After all," he reasoned,
"there was a precedent set by the year-round Christmas shops."
A year later he turned part of the shop into what he calls the
Haunted Fun Barn, "a winding path the length of a football field
[that] passes through 14 rooms and halls of a multitude of tricks
and surprises!" Now he's added an indoor miniature golf course,
with holes decorated with fanciful haunted castles occupied by
monsters and wicked witches. Familiar children's characters, including Snow White and the Seven Dwarfs, populate other holes.
And you need only look at the face of a young child playing this
fantasy golf course to realize that Farmer Friday specializes in
good family fun.

Amon Orchards, which is north of Traverse City on U.S. 31, also has fun with Halloween, so fall is the best time to stop there, when children have a chance to see the pumpkins growing on trees. Now, we adults know that pumpkins don't grow on trees, but after visiting Amon Orchards, a fair number of kids will swear we're wrong. And it is a convincing display, so don't argue with the kids. Instead, take them on a horse-drawn haywagon through the orchards. When the ride is over, let them visit the petting zoo, wander the corn maze, or take a turn pressing some cider at the antique press out front.

For adult gratification, Amon's makes wonderful, creative, sometimes-weird products, including cherry-based spaghetti sauce, cherry mustard (hot and sweet), cherry salsa, and more. Their rustic shop has samples of all these products for you to taste. Then sample a fresh apple turnover or slice of pumpkin pie.

Pumpkins, the heart of Halloween celebrations, are no more than a sideline for big fruit farms like Amon's, Robinette's, and Crane's. But they are the bread-and-butter crop of a few farmers. Darlene and Gene Rhodes, on M-43 east of Kalamazoo, label themselves the "Pumpkin People," raising enough pumpkins to "serve the needs of seven counties."

Darlene wears something orange every day and drives an orange car. They buy orange paint in five-gallon cans, and their barn, house, farm equipment, and decorative milk cans are all pumpkin orange. Their kitchen table is pumpkin shaped, complete with stem, and they share the farm with two cats, one black and the other orange. Their sideline is beef cattle — black-and-white Herefords to carry out the Halloween color theme. They say they are "orange wise, pumpkin wise, and business wise" farmers, and they are wise enough to promote their farm as a fun place to visit.

Some of that fun comes from the fact that Darlene and Gene's farm is a working farm. One woman from Battle Creek explains to the couple that she comes because "I love to smell your barn-yard." She grew up on a farm and misses it, so she visits the Rhodes' place.

Darlene and Gene create a family-style, wholesome experience for their visitors. They welcome school kids, senior citizens, and groups who want to see how a farm "works." In fact, their operation has attracted visitors from around the world, including recent visitors from Australia and Greece.

Tree-Mendus Fruit

Herb and Liz Teichman, of Tree-Mendus Fruit in Eau Claire, have labored to make it fun to stop and shop at their working farm. They've scheduled special events that span the summer: a u-pick cherry harvest in June, the International Cherry Pit-Spitting Championship in July, the "Peachy" Safari in early August, and the Harvest Moon Fruit Lovers' Weekend in late August.

They try to attract families to the farm, and for over twenty years they've had a "rent a tree" program to help them do this. Some 150 families come back year after year to pick produce from their rented trees, often having family reunions in the orchard.

One young woman from Grosse Pointe, who had been visiting the farm since she was in diapers, became engaged under the.

No one is more enthusiastic about pumpkins than
Darlene Rhodes and her husband Gene.

family tree when her fiancé gave her a ring in a hollowed-out apple. The Teichmans also have an outdoor chapel that can be used for weddings and family reunions. They'll even cater dinners for groups.

In gathering material for this book, we've enjoyed talking to the farmers who deal directly with the public, and we've learned from them a bit about the farm-fresh produce we love to eat. We've talked to them about their problems as well, and we've learned that farming is sometimes a difficult life. But most of the farmers approach the difficulties they face with a sense of humor, as you might guess from our discussion of their entertaining operations. And some farmers will entertain themselves by telling tall tales to city visitors. Our favorite stories always begin with "This is a true story . . ."

When visitors are not readily available, farmers may tell each other tall tales. One might tell another a yarn, and a new yarn will spin out of that one. Darlene Rhodes told us this true story: It is generally accepted that sunflowers cannot be transplanted. But a few years ago, Darlene had several "volunteer sunflowers," plants growing where they were not wanted from seeds dropped by birds or squirrels, and she wanted to move them. A neighboring farmer told her she could do it only if it was raining and there was thunder and lightning. Those aren't the best gardening conditions, and Darlene didn't really want to be seen outside in that kind of weather carrying her shovel, but she took the advice seriously. So on a nice day, she dug up the volunteers, sprinkled them heavily with water, and "made thunderous noises." It worked, and the dozen plants she moved all survived.

Farm animals make good stuff for stories, and many center on cows getting away and farmers chasing them. Deana Tanis, a longtime regular at the Fulton Street Farmers' Market, told us how her daughter on their Fruit Ridge Farm handled the problem: she chased them with an umbrella, which they seemed to be afraid of. She opened and closed it over and over again, and when they heard the noise, they ran right back home.

Escaping cows are a real problem in farm life, and even became a little complication for us when we were gathering information for this book. We were talking to Al Meeusen on the phone at ten o'clock one summer night — he's difficult to get a

Even a small farm stand can have a big personality.

hold of during daylight hours in the summertime — and he had to cut the conversation short. He explained that he had to go help his neighbor round up a herd of cows that had just left the barnyard.

Deana Tanis told us other animal stories that can be repeated in mixed company. She talked about the rooster "guard dog" who patroled the yard, one wing down, and attacked anybody who approached the house. She talked about the goat who liked to play "chicken" with cars and kids, charging them and swerving aside just in the nick of time. She talked about the calf, the rooster, and the St. Bernard who followed her son around the farm all day long, and who at night trooped up on the porch, wanting to follow him inside.

Our stories of farmers and farm stands only scratch the surface: there are numerous operations to visit and many entertaining farmers to meet in rural Michigan. You'll find countless farm stands, more than a hundred cider mills, and a growing number of u-pick farms. Most of the owners work creatively to make visits entertaining and pleasant.

And while some of these farm-stand operations are large and have extensive diversifications, countless other farm families have seen the need to find specific market niches and to diversify. They may not be selling a big selection of fruits and vegetables — they may have only cherries or blueberries for sale — but they may be selling a range of other items: baked goods, preserves, weaving, knitting, woodworking, carving. Again, you'll discover that it is part of the fun, and something of a surprise, to find art at a farm stand when you started out only to buy some lettuce and tomatoes for a salad.

You need only get in a car and explore some country roads to find these hundreds of stands. But to help you plan your trips, the Michigan Department of Agriculture yearly publishes *The Farm Market and U-Pick Directory*. (It can be gotten directly from the Department of Agriculture; it's also widely available at tourist information centers and farm stands.) It's a fine and helpful guide, arranged by county, but it doesn't pretend to be complete, so you'll still have the chance to find a favorite place on your own.

To the Markets

EVERYBODY HAS A FAVORITE MUNICIPAL FARM MARKET —
it's the one they go to most frequently.

The Fulton Street Farmers' Market is our "home" market, the
place where we shop two or three times a week from its opening
in May to its closing around Christmas. We have our favorite stall
for each vegetable or fruit we seek, so we've grown to know the
farmers. We trust them, and they respond by helping us choose
which item would be best for our purpose.

As we've mentioned in our Authors' Note, it's a friendly place
where we also meet and chat with friends and neighbors. And
aside from the inevitable parking jam that generates some im-
patience, we've never heard a harsh word at the Fulton Street
market.

And this atmosphere is characteristic of all the farm markets,
including Michigan's oldest and biggest, Detroit's Eastern Market,
which opened in 1892. It is among the largest farm markets in
the country.

Eastern Market (open daily except Sundays) is both a wholesale and a retail market, centering on a series of Victorian-looking
brick sheds where vendors show their wares year-round. The main
entrance to the sheds is decorously labeled "Eastern Market" in
stone, but other entrances are decorated with colorful, twelve-
foot-high cutouts of painted fruits and vegetables. With those
signs, even a first-time visitor who was still a block away could
have no doubts about what's on sale inside. Outside, farm trucks
pull up to stalls brimming with produce. These stalls line all the
aisles leading to the sheds and surround the entrances.

Buildings along the streets around the sheds are occupied by
wholesale produce vendors, specializing in everything from
bananas to nuts. Almost all the buildings are fancifully painted

Eastern Market,
Detroit

*You can find everything from radishes
to live rabbits at Eastern Market.*

with pictures of the firm's specialty — so it's not hard to figure out where to buy watermelons, for example. Wholesale meat markets, cheese stores, wine shops, bakery supply houses, wrapping-paper suppliers — all sorts of food industry businesses also cluster about the market. There's even "the Farmers Restaurant" adjacent to one of the sheds.

The density of businesses and the vast number of farm stalls make the area busy and congested. To get the full effect of that activity, visit Eastern Market early on Saturday morning. "Early" means that if you're not there by six A.M., or so we've been told, much of the best stuff will be gone. And we've noticed that by seven A.M. a number of wholesale stalls are already closed.

You have to keep an eye on the traffic. Some of the adjacent produce wholesalers also occupy space in the central sheds, and if you're a gawking tourist you have to be aware of the manic forklift drivers moving huge loads of produce between buildings. It's tough for them to see around their cargo. Making matters worse, individual farmers in their pickups and panel trucks constantly move in and out of spaces, and some of these farmers aren't great drivers. Customer vehicles add to the traffic, and there's a constant flux of shoppers in cars and trucks moving from distant parking spaces to shed entrances to load their purchases.

This bustling, hectic activity at Eastern Market makes for a happy chaos, and it's worth seeing. One guidebook to Detroit even points out that there are only three things that bring suburbanites into the city in the summer: Tiger Stadium, the Detroit Institute of Arts, and Eastern Market. We'd wager that the crowds are largest and happiest at the market, even when the Tigers are having a good year.

At Eastern Market you can buy more than produce — even live chickens and rabbits are available. And you can buy in any quantity. The egg lady will sell you a dozen eggs or a dozen crates of fifteen dozen eggs. But even though she's selling in bulk, she's still an egg lady, and like egg ladies at other farm markets, she'll wear a sweatshirt or a shirt decorated with whimsical, country-styled hens. The smallest operation is run by the honey man, who sells his wares from a card table. The stall operated by the maple-syrup man isn't much larger. By contrast, vendors who are selling bedding plants or nursery plants and supplies may occupy half-block areas.

Wholesale florists also come to Eastern Market, and most will sell at retail. Dyed German statice, for example, is available in a rainbow of colors at retail price. And we met a young artist, Alex Miller of Saint Clair, who creates wildlife sculptures, mostly of waterfowl, with his band saw and sells them to retail florists throughout the state. He first asked us if we had a store, because he quotes a different price for the trade.

Bargaining is expected here, as we learned from personal experience. We were tempted by a display of asparagus and asked the farmer the price. His response was a curt "Listen, don't squeeze me. Asparagus is a buck thirty a pound, and it's all good, young stuff." We assured him we weren't squeezing him, and handed over a five-dollar bill. He was obviously disappointed, and handed back four dollars in change. "A buck's enough for asparagus," he said, and we felt properly chastised.

So don't squeeze the farmers, but remember that price is negotiable at Eastern Market, perhaps because they do wholesale transactions or perhaps because they service a big-city community filled with people who like to bargain.

Bay City Farm Market

Bay City Farm Market (open Tuesdays and Thursdays, and Saturdays in the summertime) also has a shed, built ten years ago, but it's much like the old sheds attached to railroad stations, high roofed and open sided. That means there are no permanent stalls or displays, but the large overhangs do protect customers and farmers from rain and sun.

The shed routinely provides space for 88 vendors, but in peak season on Saturdays, when flea-market stalls and church bake sales are added, it can accommodate 110 vendors. Farmers who sell here are drawn from a broad region, including the "thumb" and the western part of the "mitten." They simply drive into the shed and set up folding tables by the open backs of their trucks.

Bay City has a few wholesalers — Weiss Fruit Market for one, which occupies three stalls — but it is primarily a retail produce market. Price is not particularly negotiable.

And unlike Eastern Market, the biggest crowds at the Bay City market come around 3:30 P.M. on Saturdays in early August, and the market stays open until early evening. Chuck's Market Restaurant, a busy, diner-like restaurant in a building adjacent to the shed (it shares space with the market office) keeps more traditional farm hours. It opens at five A.M. We met the Market Master of the Bay City Farm Market, Ralph Adams, at this restaurant. Ralph, a county employee, has been at the market only three or four years, but his predecessor was there twenty-six years. Ralph would like to stay on until retirement because, he says, "The market is such a pleasant place to be. The people around the market are so nice." He couldn't wait to introduce us to some of the farmers, choosing first a young woman selling corn and tomatoes while watching four kids with the help of her non-farming mother. "She's been coming for over twenty years, and she can really tell you about the market," Ralph said.

It turned out that she was a relative newcomer to the Bay

City market. Among those farm families who rent space by the season, the newest renter has been at the same stall for eighteen years, the oldest since 1936, the year this market opened. And this stability is common to all the farm markets we visited.

Royal Oak Market

The Royal Oak Market (open Saturdays year-round, and open additional days depending on the season) draws about 150 growers from a broad region, including the thumb and farming communities surrounding Detroit. On market days, long lines of cars wait for the limited parking space available adjacent to the market. We've found that those lines can be avoided by parking on a side street. And we've never walked more than a block or two.

The farm market is held in a huge white-washed concrete building with a covered porch area. Farmers set up displays both within the building, which they call a barn, and on the porch. The building is cavernous, but "barn" doesn't seem right for this substantial market building, and few barns have beautiful stained-glass windows depicting cornucopias of fruits and vegetables, as does this building.

The perimeter of the interior is devoted to permanent stores, giving the whole place the cheerful ambience of a flea market. Antique shops, jewelry shops, a paperback book store, bakeries (one specializing in New York–style cheesecake), a snack bar/

Visitors to the Royal Oak Market can enjoy this striking stained-glass window while choosing their produce.

restaurant, and a shop selling handmade dolls — our favorite — ring the space.

Terry Coleman has operated the doll store for twenty-two years. She specializes in soft-sculpture dolls and animals, notably cow figures in a range of humorous costumes. But we were attracted first by the creative clothes she offers for those common plastic geese, the kind that stand about two feet tall. If you own one, you can dress the thing in a tutu, a red, white, and blue outfit for the Fourth, or a witch hat and cape for Halloween. We bought the witch outfit.

One day when we were there, serious shoppers, two girls about ten years old, sat on the floor in the back of Terry's shop. While their mothers shopped for veggies, they were trying Terry's doll clothes on their own dolls. Terry was so interested and so helpful — "Have you tried this one?" she would ask — that we thought they were her own kids, until she explained, "Oh, no, but they come all the time."

Finally one of the mothers returned and bought a jar of preserves, telling us, "Terry makes the best jams in the world." At her recommendation, we bought a jar of Terry's apricot preserves.

But all the shops and the craft vendors are a mere distraction from the real business of the Royal Oak Market: the sale of produce. The most beautiful lavender eggplants we've ever seen were at Royal Oak. They were so perfect that from a distance they looked like they were ceramic. Onions in all their magnificent variety — sweet, red, bunching, Vidalia, Walla Walla, even purple onions — were the specialty of another farmer. There were corn farmers, bean farmers, and herb growers. Fruit farmers displayed their apples and apricots. In fact, you need take only one tour around the building and the porch to know why the line of cars waiting to get into the market is so long.

Lansing City Market

The Lansing City Market (open Tuesday through Saturday year-round) has about thirty-five vendors. It is housed in two connected buildings, which also afford permanent shops, although not the number or the variety that Royal Oak has. There's a French bakery, Le Boulangerie, that does all its baking on site. It unexpectedly offers knishes, a kind of Jewish potato pie, in addition to the usual bakery fare. The recipe for these knishes is "heart smart," with only five grams of fat per knish. The Upper Crust

Bread Factory also markets its baked goods here, but its ovens are at its main shop. There are also some flea market–type stores, a cheese and sausage shop, a meat shop, and the Acapulco Cafe, a Mexican-styled restaurant/snack bar.

Vendors at the Lansing City Market include the usual truck farmers, a maple-syrup man (whose prizewinning recipe for barbecued chops we include here), and, on weekends, a florist shop called Flowers and Foliage, which each month features a different perennial at its flowering peak. And since the Lansing City Market is open all year, featuring fresh produce from the South in the winter months, the grower offers amaryllis and paperwhites in December.

The Lansing and Royal Oak markets share another characteristic also common to the Kerrytown Market in Ann Arbor: you cannot buy a pound of anything — there are no scales. So you buy produce by the piece or by the basket. Instead of seeing mounds of beans, you find full-peck and half-peck boxes, artfully arranged and often on tiered steps. This gives the markets a neat, ordered look.

The Kerrytown Market (open Wednesdays and Saturdays) is an outdoor market set up on the sidewalks around the Kerrytown buildings. These house furniture shops, gift shops, a kitchen shop, restaurants, bakeries, a butcher shop, a fish store, and a marvelous year-round produce store. And if that's not enough, Zingerman's Deli, Argiero's Italian Restaurant, and the Bistro Restaurant are all within a block.

The roofing over the narrow sidewalk aisles of the market protect both shoppers and a range of weather-sensitive craft displays. Here you can find handwoven or hand-dyed textiles, cloth purses and wallets, hand-sewn clothes, inlaid wooden boxes, painted and stained wood picture frames and mirrors, dried flower arrangements, Adirondack chairs — the list goes on and varies from week to week and season to season. Remember, Ann Arbor is a university town, famous for its annual art shows, and the crafts people who display at the market are professionals who reflect the sophisticated aesthetic standards of the community.

And because Ann Arbor is a university town, this market draws a more colorful, exotic mix of shoppers than the more typical farm market. Growers satisfy the demands of these cus-

*Kerrytown
Market,
Ann Arbor*

A young family checks out the array of herbs available from Renaissance Acres at the Kerrytown Market.

tomers with equally exotic vegetables and herbs, including lemon grass and water spinach, Chinese cabbage, chickpeas, peppers, peppers, and more peppers, and odd-looking vegetables with mysterious uses.

Herb vendors range from the Renaissance Acres Herb Farm, which sells neatly packaged herbs, all organic, to the Frog Holler Organic Farmers, who sell wild bunches of mixed herbs tied together ("You should use them all together, anyhow," we were told). Countryside Herbal Foods packages their dried products as seasoning mixes and offers tastes of finished recipes. You can make a range of tasty things, as the package names indicate: Boursin Cheese, Hearty Country Bean Soup, Curried Black Bean Soup, Garden Vegetable Rice and Spice, Unbelievably HOT Peppers. Also available is their Amazing Herbal Salt Free Blend, containing seventeen ground herbs, spices, and vegetables.

A university community also seems more aware of healthy

eating habits and environmental problems, although it would be difficult to find a more environmentally aware population than farmers. So at Kerrytown, dozens of the hundred or so farmers at the market proudly proclaim their "organic farmer" status. And in season, you can buy "unsprayed" blueberries by the cup to munch while shopping.

Kalamazoo is another university town, and the Bank Street Farmers' Market has much the same feel as Kerrytown, except that it's removed from the center of town, so it doesn't have surrounding businesses and restaurants. It is open Tuesdays, Thursdays, and Saturdays during the season.

Like Kerrytown, Bank Street has roofed aisles, but there are

Bank Street Farmers' Market, Kalamazoo

You can get fresh herbs and even edible flowers from these certified organic growers at the Bank Street Farmers' Market.

few craft booths, so nothing distracts you from the offerings of the nearly two hundred farm vendors. And the quality of the produce is remarkable, from the grapes in the fall, grown at the nearby vineyards centered in Paw Paw, to the asparagus in the spring, grown extensively in Van Buren and Berrien counties. Everything is from farms within the thirteen counties surrounding Kalamazoo.

But the most unusual stall at Bank Street is run by Garling Poultry, and every other farmer at the market will tell you not to miss it. Garling sells chickens as big as small turkeys, and he has an enormous following.

Among the most colorful displays we've seen are those created by the folks of Scobey's Produce, located at one of the entrances to Bank Street. This family sells vegetables and fruit "all local grown on our farm," and shows carrots, dill, and lettuce piled high in old washtubs and huge enamel bowls.

Douglas DeLeo operates a stall at Bank Street, and he had beefsteak tomatoes weeks before we saw them anywhere else. He's been bringing produce to the market for twenty-three years, but his wife has been coming since the early fifties and is the third generation of her family to sell at the market. Her kids make the fourth, and they're helpful and knowledgeable. One of their customers told us that she's been dealing with the family "for seventy years, and they know as much as anyone."

Many of the farmers at Bank Street, like those at Kerrytown, are organic farmers, and most of them are "certified," proudly displaying their certificates. They all talk about "healing the land" and working with nature. Interest is so high in developing and sharing new methods that Kelly and Roy Jacobs, organic herb growers in Delton, told us that they and other organic farmers have a barter fair every September to swap herbs and share experiences.

Herbs and "edible flowers" are the stock of East Branch Specialty Farms; their stall is run by Susan Brennan Barnes and Lilli Congdon. Susan, a psychologist, comes to Bank Street as a kind of therapy. "The market's such a social thing," she told us, and she loves to share "finds" with customers.

In the summertime Traverse City runs an outdoor market on Wednesdays and Saturdays in a parking lot alongside the Boardman River. About fifty farmers sell produce under a blue canopy. The market opens at eight A.M., but farmers attracted from as far away as the thumb and the upper peninsula may still be unloading at that hour. It's a good idea to get there reasonably early, though, because many farmers will be gone by one in the afternoon.

In Traverse City, "The Cherry Capital of the World," you expect to find cherries in season, but that's not the only crop available. The fruit orchards also grow peaches, plums, pears, nectarines, and apples. Berry growers offer red and black raspberries, blackberries, and thimbleberries. And sweet corn is particularly sweet this far north.

Traverse City

Grand Haven has a small outdoor farm market at Chinook Pier on the Grand River. Here, as in Traverse City, the produce shopper can see the masts of sailboats going by, or walk a few paces to see the large charter fishing boats rocking at the pier. From June to October, on Wednesdays and Saturdays about twenty growers come to Grand Haven to sell produce under the colorful canvas roof.

Grand Haven

Some of the growers at Grand Haven also come to the Fulton Street Farmers' Market in Grand Rapids. It's a block-long outdoor farm market that extends between Fulton Street and Fountain Street. It's open on Tuesdays, Wednesdays, Fridays, and Saturdays.

Fulton Street Farmers' Market, Grand Rapids

The Fulton Street market has more of a farm-market feel than most. The cement aisle is flanked by permanent, weathered tables, but there is no roof or canopy. Farmers rig a variety of colorful tarps to protect the aisle and their produce, and the individuality of the farmer comes through in the choices. A blueberry farmer, for example, will use a blue plastic tarp, a wise aesthetic choice: you've never seen bluer-looking blueberries.

The Fulton Street market is marked for 122 stalls, and during peak season all are rented. As many as 107 farmers reserve space all season, and the remaining booths are used by crafts people, bakeries, and nonprofit organizations that rent space on a daily basis for fundraising activities.

This market is extremely popular; residents can't seem to get enough fresh fruits and vegetables. So on Thursdays, when the Fulton Street market is closed, about twenty of the farmers bring produce to the Monroe Mall in downtown Grand Rapids. That outdoor mall is busiest when the office workers take their lunch

*The Fulton Street Farmers' Market, our "home" market,
has fine produce and friendly farmers.*

hour, so at noontime on Thursdays you'll see men and women in power suits buying onions and carrots for dinner, and perhaps a bouquet of flowers for a secretary's desk. Fresh-baked breads are also popular items at the downtown market.

Holland Municipal Farm Market

The Holland Municipal Farm Market at the Holland Civic Center is another large outdoor market. (It's open Wednesdays and Saturdays during the growing season.) But for this market the city provides little more than an open parking lot, hardly even marking out areas for stalls. Farmers set up folding tables in a variety of configurations to suit their own needs, and provide tent-like tarps and umbrellas, or not, as they see fit.

And since this is in the center of Michigan's best fruit area, almost a hundred farmers come regularly, and with great pride. When we drive the back roads of the area and stop at individual farm stands, farmers frequently advise us to visit their stalls at the market in Holland, just to get a feel for the abundance the region produces. It's wonderful, they tell us.

These farmers really feel they belong to something good, and the customers share that feeling. Both they and the farmers reflect the tidy and conservative community around Holland. Even the herb farmer, Mary Hoogerhyde from Borculo, is neat and clean, unlike some of the neo-hippies at other markets. We stopped to buy a bunch of fresh tansy to dry, and Mary told us that the yellow flowers that had a domed button shape would do better dried than those that were already flat. But when we asked what else tansy was good for, she giggled before she responded that "you could make a tea from the leaves that's good for female problems."

At Mary's umbrella, we ran into Nancy Banaitis, the chef for the Van Andel family. Nancy, who summers in Holland, thinks nothing can compare to "her market" in Holland, even though she also shops the Fulton Street market and farm stands.

This may be because Holland is the simplest market of all

A young boy helps out at the Holland Municipal Farm Market.

the major farm markets we've visited — the one with apparently the fewest restrictions and the one where the farmer's individuality can show the most.

So Holland's farm market is clearly a good one, although it's not our favorite, as you know from our previous comments. Your favorite may be one we've never visited; there's got to be fifty or more around the state, ranging in size from two or three farmers at a rural intersection to some almost as large as the major markets we've discussed. Our advice? Visit one or more markets and become a regular shopper there. It's one of the most pleasant ways to enjoy fresh Michigan fruit and vegetables, the world's best foods.

SPRING

IT IS THE TIME OF CHANGE, AN EXCITING TIME PROMIS-
ing new life to come. Intermittent thaws first soften and then
compress the snow pack, revealing brown patches of ground,
stalks of withered grass, and bare shrubs. Refreezing and light,
wet snows turn the remaining snow cover into a glistening,
rounded meringue. Some farmers report that they can scrape the
snow from their kitchen gardens and find fresh mint leaves, ready
for harvest.

Gray winter days start to give way to sunny days, and with
cool nights, the sap starts to flow. That means it's sugar bush time,
perhaps as early as late February, and traditionally that's the first
farm activity of spring.

Farmers leave their warm living rooms and brave the still-
chilly winds of spring to tap the hard maples in the wood lot or
lining the edges of the rural roads. For many of us, the first real
signs of spring are not the robins but the galvanized pails hanging
from the trees and the hand-lettered signs and banners by farm
driveways proclaiming "Maple Syrup for Sale."

Maple Syrup

Farm families who tap trees may literally move into their
sugar shacks, where they keep oak- or maple-slab fires going to
evaporate the sap. It's almost like going to camp, and sugar-shack
chili is one of their favorite meals. We've included a recipe for it
here.

It takes about forty to fifty gallons of boiled-down sap to
form one gallon of syrup. But this varies greatly with the season.
Dona Maier, of Maier's Sugar Bush in Caledonia, says, "One year
we had to boil 103 gallons to get just one of syrup. It wasn't much
fun that year."

Maple syrup production has become a big industry, with an
estimated 100,000 gallons produced in Michigan alone, and it's

These pails are a clear sign that it's sugar-bush time.

hard work to produce that much. The Maiers tap 1,000 trees, which, in a good year, yield about 400 gallons of syrup.

Maple syrup that's marketed through farm stands or municipal farm markets is a pure product, devoid of additives like preservatives and colorings. Most farmers will have batches that range in flavor, so ask for a taste or ask about the grade. The grade A syrup, considered the highest quality, is the lightest in color and flavor, although all the syrup has the same sugar content, 66 percent by weight.

The Maiers use some of their syrup to make maple cream, a spread for toast; maple sugar, to be used wherever brown sugar is used; and an assortment of maple candies. The Maiers sell all this at the Sugar Bush, a cozy country store decorated with great pictures of sugar-shack activities. Because it's right next door to their farmhouse, the Maiers often leave the Sugar Bush unattended. You browse their wares and then let them know via intercom when you're ready to buy. Dona or one of her children or grandchildren will come to help and to chat. By the way, this is a great place to bring children. The Maiers have samples of all the sweets for tasting, and children just love these spring treats (as will you).

Because of its high sugar content, plain maple syrup is a stable product, with long shelf life in the kitchen. If you don't refrigerate it after opening, it may mold. But even that doesn't hurt its quality, although most people balk at the thought of spreading mold on pancakes. Simply fish the mold out; the remaining syrup will still be good. Dodd's Sugar Shack in Niles suggests that you boil the syrup for three minutes and store it in a clean container to keep the mold from coming back. Should the syrup cloud, clarity can also be restored by boiling it for a few minutes, cooling it to room temperature, and then rebottling it.

Maple syrup is usually used straight, as a topping for pancakes and waffles, or as a topping for fresh fruit cups or salads. Try it also as a sauce for ice cream, cake, or even vanilla pudding.

Maple syrup's unique flavor offers other creative possibilities. One farmer said she uses maple syrup in her bread recipe, "a cup per batch." When we asked her what she meant by "batch," she said it was two large loaves. You can also substitute maple syrup for sugar in a recipe for barbecue sauce, and your spareribs will have championship quality. We've included a recipe from Wesley N. Clark, of Clark's Sugar Bush, that took second place at the Saginaw Fair.

You can dribble maple syrup over cooked carrots, squash, or sweet potatoes. You can use it to flavor a ham loaf. Or you can use maple syrup in a glaze for your ham, roast duck, or goose. Combine it with cherries, and you can make delightfully different versions of traditional dishes.

Flats of flowers provide a welcome breath of spring.

Bedding Plants

Another sign that spring has arrived is the announcement by greenhouse farmers and plant nurseries that flats of bedding plants are ready for sale. In early spring, Ludema's in Kentwood is awash with flats of primroses in full bloom — blues, yellows, and reds mostly, and combinations as well. They're ready to take home and enjoy as a touch of color in the house; then, after the danger of frost is over, they can be planted outside. Pansies seem to be "frost hardy" and are planted shallowly, so they can be thrown into the ground almost at first thaw. Koetsier Greenhouse on the outskirts of Grand Rapids has flats of them and the smaller Johnny-jump-ups ready for planting. It also starts showing hanging baskets in early spring.

At this point it's a little early to consider tomatoes and peppers, but you can see the plants started at Wm. Bos Greenhouses, just across the road from Koetsier's.

This bedding-plant industry has approached a wholesale trade of 100 million dollars, with hundreds of farmers sharing the pot. In mid-May, Detroit's Eastern Market schedules a bedding-plant day, the world's largest such event, which attracts farmers and buyers from neighboring Canada as well as Michigan.

Most municipal farm markets open for business around the first of May, and bedding plants are a prominent part of the early stock. Even the market's "egg lady" will have a few flats for sale. But the real excitement comes with the appearance of piles of fresh green asparagus.

Asparagus

Asparagus that's imported from warmer states may appear in supermarkets and produce stores in January, and it's welcome. But Michigan asparagus, freshly snapped, is worth celebrating. "Snapped" is important. Asparagus is best when it's broken off in the field, when the stalk snaps at the point where its woody stem gives way to the tender, new growth.

So look for stalks with irregular, broken bottoms. It doesn't seem to matter, in terms of flavor, whether you select pencil-thin stalks or stalks as thick as your thumb. Whichever you prefer, select stalks that are of uniform diameter so all cook at the same rate.

Asparagus has become virtually an object of veneration, and its worshipers have devised, and swear by, dozens of ways to cook it. All agree that it is best served within a day of purchase. It may be boiled rapidly, or simmered slowly. It may be steamed vertically in a special asparagus steamer, or horizontally in a fish poacher. It may be microwaved. It may be baked in foil so that it cooks only in its own juices.

One effective, easy method is to cook asparagus in a skillet large enough to hold all the stalks in a single layer. Bring lightly salted water to a rapid boil and drop in the asparagus, then reduce the heat to a simmer. If you have neatly cut off the irregular snapped ends (you'll lose only a quarter-inch doing this), cook these pieces in the boiling water before adding the stalks. This adds a little flavor to the water and inhibits some leaching of flavor from the tender stalks.

Farmers say asparagus is done cooking when it's tender. And

although some people express a preference for al-dente vegetables, melt-in-the-mouth asparagus is the tradition.

It's so delicious plain that most people just eat asparagus hot from the stove, with a little butter and salt on top. But the flavor also lends itself to a variety of sauces. Try asparagus with lemon

Asparagus — the quintessential spring vegetable

butter or topped with a mild mustard sauce. Toss cooked asparagus together with pasta and seasoned olive oil for a pasta primavera. Eat it at room temperature with a simple oil-and-vinegar dressing. Or try the Asparagus Provençal recipe we've included here. We serve this often as a first course, and it's a spectacular dish to take to potlucks.

Shed a tear when asparagus season is over, but know that most farmers agree that, if you're going to freeze anything, you should freeze asparagus. And again, there are a variety of methods. Marge Geukes at the Fulton Street Farmers' Market advised us to "blanch the asparagus in boiling water until it 'changes color,' about a minute or less. Dry it carefully, and freeze it in a single layer on wax paper or cookie sheets." She stores it in tightly sealed, double-plastic bags, and reports that individual stalks can be easily separated for cooking.

Snow peas appear at market just when asparagus begins to fade out. Again, they're a real sign of spring, and they may be cooked by steaming, boiling, or sautéing. We've included an idea for stir-fried snow peas in our recipes. Also remember that raw pea pods make good dippers for your favorite dip or can be stuffed like celery.

Snow Peas

Rhubarb doesn't generate the same excitement as asparagus, but it comes along at about the same time, or even a little earlier. It's often called "pie-plant" and is considered the "first fruit" of spring, although it isn't a fruit. Yet it's not a common vegetable at farm markets, perhaps because there's not much to be done with rhubarb except cover its taste with lots of sugar and serve it in a pie. But rhubarb does have a slight laxative effect. The farmers who sell it, mostly older, grandmotherly types, swear by eating rhubarb and benefiting from the cleansing effect it has on the body's system as a purifying rite of spring. And if you need mid-winter purification, rhubarb does freeze well.

Rhubarb

Farmers often just stew rhubarb in sugar and water, eating it as a vegetable or simple dessert, but we've included an elegant recipe for Rhubarb Crisp, best served topped with maple-pecan ice cream.

Rhubarb-strawberry pie is another Michigan spring specialty, and the seasons of the two pie ingredients do overlap. Michigan strawberries are small and juicy, better tasting than their California cousins, and reach the market in late spring and early summer.

Strawberries

Strawberries are the first real fruits of summer, though with the development of ever-bearing varieties they have become a summer-long treat. But nothing tastes better than the first berries, which farmers display in their wooden berry baskets in spring and early summer.

Select strawberries that are fully red — firm, glistening berries. Rinse them and eat them as they are. For a special treat, cut off the hulls and serve the strawberries English style, with clotted cream, accompanied by a simple cookie.

These first strawberries need no sugar. In fact, if you top cereal with fresh berries, the kids will even eat the good-for-you, low-sugar varieties. They'll complain and still demand their favorite (heavily advertised) sweet cereal, but they'll eat their breakfast.

Adults like sweets too, and you can make candy out of strawberries. Chocolate-dipped strawberries are the simplest and most elegant of desserts, and you can prepare them at the last minute. Just melt some semisweet chocolate and add some flavored liqueur — Grand Marnier, for example. (Proportions aren't important. If your mix gets gloppy, add more liqueur; if it's runny, just heat it a while longer.) Select the largest berries and dip them in the warm mixture, then chill them on wax paper until firm. Take this approach even further and invite friends to a party designed around the delicacy. Simply serve a traditional European cheese fondue, with veggies and bread cubes to dip, and a large pot of chocolate fondue for dessert, with strawberries and cake cubes to dip. (We've included fondue recipes here.)

When perfect, tiny strawberries are available, it's also time to start a big jar of brandied tutti-frutti. Remember to add more perfect fruit to the jar through the seasons, as each variety reaches its peak. We've included an old family recipe for this concoction. And we like to eat it through the winter as a topping for ice cream.

Cook imaginatively with strawberries. Cook chicken breasts with strawberries, ham steaks glazed with strawberries — cook anything that might benefit by being served with a sweet sauce. But don't ignore everybody's favorite use for strawberries: a good, old-fashioned strawberry shortcake. Every farmer has a recipe for this dessert; one of the easiest uses biscuits as the base. You simply sugar the strawberries, mash half of them, and mound the mix on

A sign that spring is yielding to summer — quarts of juicy strawberries at the farm market

a biscuit half. Then you add the other biscuit half, top with the remaining berries, and bury the whole concoction in whipped cream. Dona Maier always adds a dollop of maple syrup.

Every farmer also knows how to make strawberry preserves and jams, and some sell them to help you get through the winter. Other farmers swear by strawberry freezer jams. All the commercial pectin products and thickeners, including a new low-sugar product called Garden Fare, come with packaged recipes.

If you want to make cooked preserves following an old family recipe, please consult a current book on canning first. We've also included a warning and a suggestion about canning in our Early Summer section.

Fresh strawberries freeze nicely just as they are. Just hull and wash the berries, perhaps cutting large ones in half, then dry well before freezing them on trays. If you serve them while they're still slightly frozen, they'll keep their shape, and the flavor will be fine.

Potted herbs begin to appear at farm markets in late spring, and they can give stored winter vegetables a new taste. Fresh parsley will help the potatoes, and chives will liven the taste of everything. Rosemary and oregano can be sprinkled on most vegetable and meat dishes.

Also, don't forget that the big municipal farm markets have flowers in the spring — bunches of lily of the valley, daffodils, and tulips. These are beautiful, but to really celebrate spring, take home some forsythia branches for forcing, or buy some pussy-willow canes.

SPRING RECIPES

Sugar Shack Chili

SERVES TEN

This recipe comes from Peggy Cove of P Weavings Plus and L. Mawby Vineyards in Suttons Bay. She says this is "a good, hearty meal to be enjoyed when making maple syrup. Sugar Shack Chili can be kept for hours, even days, in a sugar shack." She suggests L. Mawby M. Foch as the wine to drink with the chili.

1½ cups bacon and/or small ham chunks, fried crisp
2 quarts tomato sauce
1 small onion, chopped
5 medium shallots, chopped
1 cup fresh Jerusalem artichokes, diced
1 15-ounce can kidney beans
2 cups potato puree
2 cups L. Mawby M. Foch wine
2 tablespoons dried parsley
1 tablespoon thyme
1 tablespoon oregano
3 tablespoons chili powder
4 tablespoons maple syrup

Combine all the ingredients in a large pot. Heat to boiling, and then simmer for 45 minutes to an hour. Serve piping hot, with crusty bread or rolls.

Creamy Asparagus Soup

MAKES ABOUT 2½ QUARTS

This recipe from Shirley Beachum won first prize at the National Asparagus Food Show. Shirley owns a farm in Shelby with the wonder-

ful name of "Farm Fresh Asparagus," which certainly tells you what she grows.

Shirley says she likes to blanch and freeze asparagus in portions just right for this recipe, so she can make her favorite soup all year.

¼ cup butter or margarine
2 medium onions, chopped
2 cups celery, chopped
3 cups raw asparagus, grated
1 clove garlic, minced
½ cup all-purpose flour
4 cups chicken broth
½ teaspoon dried thyme
½ teaspoon dried marjoram
3 large potatoes, peeled and cut into ½-inch cubes
4 cups milk
4 cups fresh or frozen asparagus, cut in 1-inch pieces
salt and pepper to taste
sliced almonds
shredded cheddar cheese
chopped fresh tomato

In a Dutch oven, melt the butter, then sauté the onions, celery, grated asparagus, and garlic until tender. Stir in the flour, then add the chicken broth, herbs, and potatoes. Cook over low heat, stirring occasionally, until the soup is thickened and the potatoes are tender, about thirty minutes.

Then add the milk, the asparagus pieces, and the salt and pepper. You want to heat the soup until the asparagus turns a bright green color, but avoid bringing the mixture to a hard boil, or the milk will curdle. Garnish with the almonds, cheese, and tomato.

Asparagus Provençal

SERVES SIX

This makes a beautiful spring salad or first course, with the bright-green asparagus stalks, red tomatoes, and black olives providing strik-

ing color contrast. *It's great to take to a potluck supper because it's served at room temperature.*

    2 pounds asparagus
    2 tablespoons wine vinegar
    2 teaspoons Dijon mustard
    ¼ cup olive oil
    2 green onions, minced
    2 plum tomatoes, seeded and diced
    ⅓ cup Nicoise olives
    1 tablespoon capers, drained
       salt and pepper to taste

Cook the asparagus until tender, about five minutes. Drain well and cool on ice, then let stand at room temperature.

Whisk the vinegar and mustard together, and gradually whisk in the olive oil. Then add the green onions, tomatoes, olives, and capers. Season with salt and pepper to taste. Arrange the asparagus stalks on a platter, spoon over the dressing, and serve.

Authors' note: You can substitute fresh whole green beans or a steamed head of cauliflower for the asparagus.

Snow Peas and Mushrooms

SERVES TWO

We like this as a side dish when we splurge, forget about cholesterol, and broil a steak. We also cut a tomato in half, dress the halves with a little olive oil, some garlic salt, a sprinkle of oregano, and some Parmesan cheese, and broil them with the steak. It makes a pretty plate.

    1 tablespoon margarine or butter
    4 ounces fresh mushrooms, sliced
    4 ounces snow peas, with the ends trimmed
       salt and pepper to taste

Melt the margarine in a nonstick skillet. Quickly cook the mushrooms until they get soft and the sugar peas until they're tender but still crisp. Salt and pepper to taste.

Sauté of Six Vegetables

SERVES TWO TO THREE

When we saw Nancy Banaitis at the Holland Municipal Farm Market, she introduced us to Gert Eding, the farmer who grows the bok choy Nancy uses in so many of the dishes she creates. The two of them bubbled over with ideas for using this celery, and Nancy told us, "I'll send you a simple recipe using celery you'll just love." It turned out to be this sauté.

Nancy is the chef for the family of Jay Van Andel, cofounder of the Amway Corporation of Ada.

>   a few tablespoons peanut oil
> ¼ cup green onion, sliced on the bias
> ½ cup bok choy, sliced across the head into inch-wide strips
> ½ cup Napa celery, sliced across the head into inch-wide strips
> ½ cup asparagus, cut into 2-inch sticks
> 1 tablespoon garlic, diced fine
> 1 teaspoon ginger root, minced
> ½ cup snow peas, strings removed
> 1 3-ounce can bamboo shoots, drained
> ¼ cup carrots, sliced into 2-inch matchsticks
> ½ teaspoon sesame oil

Heat a wok, then add the peanut oil and green onion. It's important to add the next three ingredients in this order: the bok choy, the Napa celery, and the asparagus. Stir quickly for one minute, then add the garlic, ginger root, snow peas, bamboo shoots, and carrots. Stir quickly again, while adding the sesame oil. Cook over medium heat until the veggies are done to taste.

Chef Banaitis says, "This is a basic recipe. Add other vegetables in season — green beans, broccoli, or cabbage — and add roast pork slices, chicken, or shrimp."

European Cheese Fondue

SERVES THREE TO FOUR

The directions for this fondue suggest that you use the classic Swiss combination of Emmenthaler and Gruyère cheeses. But we make it with just about any leftover cheese we have, except for the new low-fat or nonfat cheeses — they just don't seem to melt well.

And one night, when the party had been going for a long time, we tried to thin the thickened fondue by adding more wine. That doesn't work: we were left with a ball of cheese swimming in the newly added wine.

¾ pound cheese (Emmenthaler and Gruyère) cut into
   small cubes
2 tablespoons flour
1½ cup dry white wine
1 tablespoon lemon juice
1 garlic clove, slashed
   salt and freshly ground black pepper to taste
3 tablespoons kirsch

Toss the cheese cubes and the flour together in a plastic bag until the cubes are thoroughly coated. Pour the wine and the lemon juice into a fondue pot, then add the garlic clove. Heat the liquid until it bubbles, and discard the garlic. Then add the cheese a little at a time while stirring constantly with a fork, until all the cheese is added and the mixture is smooth. Salt and pepper to taste, and stir in the kirsch. Keep it warm for serving.

The classic way to eat fondue is to dip crusty French bread cubes in the cheese, using fondue forks. We like dipping fresh, in-season vegetables, either slightly parboiled or raw. Try snow peas in the spring, broccoli and cauliflower in the fall.

Maple Barbecued Spareribs

SERVES FOUR

Wesley N. Clark, of Clark's Sugar Bush in Mason, was willing to share his secret ingredient with us. He uses apricot nectar instead of water when he parboils his spareribs before baking them. With this recipe, he took second place at the Saginaw Fair.

- 4 pounds spareribs
- 1 large can apricot nectar
- ¾ cup pure maple syrup
- 1 tablespoon tomato catsup
- 1 tablespoon cider vinegar
- 1 tablespoon onion, finely chopped
- 1 tablespoon Worchestershire sauce
- 1 teaspoon salt
- ¼ teaspoon dry mustard
- ⅛ teaspoon black pepper

Place spareribs in a large pot and add enough apricot nectar to cover. Bring to a boil, then reduce the heat and simmer for thirty minutes. Next drain the spareribs and transfer them to a baking dish. Mix all the other ingredients together and pour about half of this mixture over the spareribs.

Bake the ribs in a 350° oven for thirty minutes or until they're tender. Turn and baste them with the remaining sauce occasionally while baking. To finish the browning, broil the ribs for five minutes after the baking.

Country Veal

SERVES FOUR

Roberta Jacobson describes all her recipes as "a taste of northern Michigan." She and her husband, Mike, are proud of their Leelanau Cellars Wines from Omena, and this recipe features their Spring Splendor or Winter White wine.

1½ pounds top-round veal steak
flour
1½ tablespoons cooking oil
½ teaspoon salt
⅛ teaspoon pepper
½ teaspoon garlic salt
½ teaspoon paprika
½ teaspoon dry mustard
¼ teaspoon Worcestershire sauce
⅛ teaspoon dried rosemary
1 tablespoon catsup
½ cup Leelanau Cellars wine, either Spring Splendor or Winter White
½ cup sour cream
parsley
1 tomato, cut in wedges

Cut the veal into serving-size pieces and dredge with flour. In a Dutch oven, brown on both sides in heated oil. Combine all the ingredients except the sour cream, parsley, and tomato, and stir until blended. Pour over the browned veal, then cover and simmer until tender, about 40 to 50 minutes. Arrange the veal on a platter and keep it warm. Add the sour cream to the drippings in the pan and heat through but do not boil. Pour the mixture over the meat, and garnish with the parsley and the tomato wedges.

Authors' note: Serve this dish with the same wine used in the preparation. (It's best to avoid using "cooking wine." If it's worth making, it's worth using good ingredients.)

Warm Rhubarb Crisp with Hudsonville French Vanilla Bean or Maple Walnut Ice Cream

SERVES FOUR

This recipe appeared in the Spring 1993 issue of Michigan Wine Country. *Joe Borrello, a well-known wine expert who is the editor of that magazine, let us share this springtime recipe created by Scott Gilbert, Executive Chef of the Amway Grand Plaza Hotel in Grand Rapids.*

RHUBARB MIXTURE:
2 eggs
2 tablespoons milk
½ cup sugar
3 tablespoons flour
½ teaspoon nutmeg
3 cups rhubarb, chopped

Combine the first five ingredients and toss with the rhubarb. Next put the mixture in an 8 x 8-inch glass baking dish that's been greased.

STREUSEL TOPPING:
½ stick butter
⅓ cup brown sugar
⅓ cup granulated sugar
½ cup bread flour
1 tablespoon cinnamon
½ cup chopped nuts

Let the butter get a bit soft. Then add the brown sugar, the granulated sugar, the bread flour, and the cinnamon, and blend with a fork until the mixture is crumbly. Stir the nuts into the topping, and then sprinkle it over the rhubarb mixture. Bake at 350° for 20 to 30 minutes, or until the rhubarb mixture is bubbling and the top is golden brown. When cool, serve it topped with the ice cream.

Authors' note: Chef Gilbert suggests that you serve this dessert with either a sparkling wine or a Michigan late-harvest Johannisburg Riesling.

Easy Chocolate Fondue, American Style

MAKES ENOUGH SAUCE FOR A PINT OF FRUIT

This is a wonderful dipping sauce for pieces of fresh fruit. Strawberries in spring and early summer are good, but so are apple slices and pears in the fall. This makes a perfect cocktail or party snack.

- 1 6-ounce package semisweet chocolate morsels
- 2 tablespoons water
- 2 tablespoons whipping cream
- 2 tablespoons brandy or flavored liqueur

Combine the chocolate and water in a heated double boiler and stir until the chocolate is melted and the mixture is smooth. Then add the whipping cream and the brandy, stirring until the mix is again smooth. Keep it warm over hot water and dip your fruit.

For variations, try adding a dash of cinnamon or a teaspoon of instant coffee.

Fresh Berries with Florio Zabaglione

Zabaglione is the traditional Italian dessert, and John Russo, of G. B. Russo & Son in Grand Rapids, raves about this version, which uses Florio Sweet Marsala from Italy. We don't know of a Michigan-made marsala.

SERVES SIX

- 8 eggs, separated
- ⅛ teaspoon cream of tartar
- 1 cup confectioners' sugar
- ⅓ cup Florio Sweet Marsala
- 1 teaspoon pure vanilla extract
- 2 cups fresh berries (strawberries, raspberries, or blueberries)

Beat the egg whites with the cream of tartar until they're stiff but not dry. Briefly whisk the egg yolks with the sugar in a large metal bowl, set over a saucepan of simmering water, for about two minutes, or until the mixture thickens and is lemon colored. Then whisk in the marsala and vanilla and continue whisking for about three minutes, until the mixture is light and almost doubled in volume. Last, fold in the beaten egg whites. Then divide the zabaglione into serving bowls and sprinkle with the fresh berries.

This dessert really takes no longer than ten or fifteen minutes to prepare, and you will have something quite special to serve your guests.

Tutti Frutti or Brandied Fruit

To make this one, you have to start in the spring with the little Michigan strawberries. Be sure your container is big enough, and that you have a cool place to store it. After years of using a crock, I now use a two-gallon glass jar with a wide mouth, and store it in the fridge to keep away fruit flies — they love it too.

1 quart brandy

Add, as they come in season, about five varieties of perfect fruit:

1 quart strawberries
1 quart cherries, pitted
1 quart raspberries
1 quart peaches, peeled and sliced
1 quart pineapple chunks, peeled

These are my favorites, but you can also use currants, gooseberries, and apricots — but not apples, bananas, and pears; they get too mushy. Grape skins get tough, so you probably shouldn't use grapes, either.

With each fruit you use, add an equal amount of sugar. Stir every day, until all the fruit is in and all the sugar is dissolved.

The Tutti Frutti will keep indefinitely and remind you of summer all winter long. We use it as a topping for ice cream, cake, and puddings.

EARLY SUMMER

EARLY SUMMER HAS THE BRILLIANCE OF A RED, WHITE, and blue fireworks display. The gray skies of winter are forgotten, and the pastels of the misty, rainy, foggy days of spring give way to bright blue skies. Towering, solid-white clouds give depth to the skies and carry the threat of summer thunderstorms, which, when they burst, cool the fields of scarlet tomatoes ripening during the long, pleasant days.

Worries about killing frosts are gone, and temperatures are consistently warm, but there is little sign yet of the sustained, oppressive heat of August. Early summer is the best of times. It is the time to be outdoors. It is the time to play baseball. It is the time to ride your bike. And early summer is the time to work in your garden. The farm markets and farm stands are still loaded with flats of annuals, and they've reduced the prices. Interesting new varieties of perennials appear, promising years of beauty and not much work. Favorites among perennials in Michigan are day-lilies, flowers that come in different sizes, colors, and blooming times.

Perennials

Michigan has a unique daylily farm, Englerth Gardens in Hopkins, which is run by Mary Herrema and her husband, Kenneth (Mary's parents started the farm). They themselves have developed many of the daylilies that they ship to markets around the country. Every Saturday in July, Englerth Gardens holds an open house, and you can see a thousand different varieties in full bloom in demonstration gardens, so you'll know just how the flowers will look in your home garden. The Herremas offer free lectures and demonstrations about daylilies and the other perennials they grow, although they admit that daylilies will grow in any kind of well-drained soil and in sun or partial shade. They'll thrive for years with minimal care.

The Herremas are environmentally conscious, and they've kept part of their farm planted with local species. So when you visit Englerth Gardens, make time to explore the acres of wild-flower fields that surround the gardens, and listen to other presentations about the use of medicinal herbs and other plants.

Every year the Herremas also help one public charity or institution to create gardens, so this gives you a chance to see how their perennials look at other sites. They recently replanted part of the grounds of the Brookby estate in East Grand Rapids, designed and planted a garden for the Grand Rapids Public Library, and planted the grounds of the Ronald McDonald House in Grand Rapids. The Herremas are nice people.

Perennials, including daylilies, and flats of annuals are a small part of the excitement at farm markets. The full promise of spring is delivered in early summer, when seemingly every day some new fruit or vegetable makes its annual return to market.

Cherries

By the Fourth of July, Michigan cherries hit the markets. Black sweet cherries, bing cherries, Queen Anne cherries, Montmorency cherries, tart cherries — Michigan has them all. Cherries come in first in the southern part of the state, but Traverse City is recognized as the "Cherry Capital of the World."

Hundreds of farm stands in the Traverse City area open for the five or six weeks of the season, offering washed sweet cherries to travelers. You can't stop at every stand, but if you're in the area, you will stop at some. Eat the sweet, juicy cherries by the handful, being careful not to dribble them on your white shirt. The juice isn't as easy to get out as detergent ads would like you to believe.

After you've had your fill of the fresh fruit, consider the multiple uses for cherries created by the imaginative growers and processors. The simplest is the cherry juice sold at the Cherry Hut in Beulah. People drive miles out of their way just for a drink of that juice. Benjamin Twiggs, Inc., which operates two shops in Traverse City, has a mail-order catalog listing twenty-five different products, from cherry preserves to "Rich n' Tangy Cherry Steak Sauce" and "Cherriyaki Marinade." Amon Orchards (north of Traverse City on U.S. 31) offers a similar range of products, including a hot-and-sweet cherry mustard and a cherry spaghetti sauce. The nationally renowned and prize-winning American Spoon Company makes some of the best preserves in the world,

*A few quarts of farm-fresh cherries are
a delicious way to welcome summer.*

including its "Spoon Fruits" — preserves with no added sugar. It advertises these preserves as "summer in the jar," and its fresh-tasting Cherry Spoon Fruit supports that slogan. American Spoon is also among the most active promoters of dried Michigan cherries. Use them like raisins — put them on cereal, in salads, and in baked goods.

In late June, cherry pies, cherry tarts, and cherry muffins begin to replace the strawberry baked goods at markets. In the Traverse City region, Underwood Orchards sells a locally famous and coveted sweet-tart cherry pie. The recipe is a closely guarded secret, so you'll just have to buy one there. It's worth making the trip to the Old Mission Peninsula, north of the city, and the views are great.

Liz Teichman of Tree-Mendus Fruit in Eau Claire does have a hint for cherry pies. "I add lemon juice to my blueberry pies to balance the sweetness," she says, "and I add blueberries to my tart cherry pies to balance the tartness."

The most unique bakery we've found is on the other side of the state in the thumb. Mary Salmonowicz, the owner of Mary's Pie Shop in Lexington, the heart of orchard country, makes luscious fruit and berry pies using local produce as it comes into season.

She was inspired by the farm wives in Lancaster, Pennsylvania, who sold baked goods out of their kitchens, so she bakes her pies in the small kitchen of a small farmhouse, in a regular home oven only big enough to bake two or three pies at a time. "It's just the way mother did it," she says, and Mary uses her mother's secret dough recipe to go with the fresh fruit she purchases from neighboring farms. Three of those neighbors stopped in to buy pies during the short while we were in the shop.

U-Pick

There are concrete advantages to using u-pick farms to get your fruit. Usually u-pick prices are cheaper, so you'll save money. You'll know absolutely that your pickings are fresh. And you'll know that the fruit you picked came from Michigan.

But there are minor hazards. John Mann of Fennville, who operates a u-pick farm and brings produce to the Holland Municipal Farm Market, told us of the day three ladies stopped to pick raspberries. "They had picked barely a pint each when they had to quit, complaining about their aching backs. We pick seven or eight hours a day. Think how they'd have felt then," he grinned.

It seemed to us that picking raspberries might also present problems with thorns, and we asked John how the three ladies managed that. He smilingly told us that domesticated plants have only "little bitty stickers," and that was no problem. When he showed us his heavily calloused hands, we could see why he thought there was no problem. But John did think that you'd be more comfortable if you wore a long-sleeved shirt for raspberry picking.

Blueberries

Blueberry picking is perhaps the easiest u-pick activity. The bushes grow tall enough so that you can pick without bending over (unless that one perfect berry is on a bottom branch), there are no thorns to contend with, and it's easy to tell which berries are ripe for picking.

It's so easy, in fact, that we feel we have to warn you of a minor hazard. U-pick blueberries multiply on the drive home. The first time we went picking, we did so with calm deliberation, choosing only those berries that were fully ripe and the size of small grapes. We filled a small, shallow bucket provided by the farm, figuring that we'd have enough berries to sprinkle on a couple of bowls of cereal and perhaps a few bowls of ice cream. When we got home, we discovered that the small bucketful had grown, and we had plenty for our immediate needs and so many left over that we filled our counter-height freezer.

Brita Soper, who owns the Blueberry Patch in Sawyer, told us of another hazard in blueberry picking. She recalled the day a family from Chicago came to pick. (Chicago people are frequent visitors there, and after driving down the quarter-mile narrow dirt road to reach the Sopers' large u-pick farm, they really feel they're in the country.) On this particular day, a neighbor's goat had managed to get through the fence. "He was doing that all the time," Brita says. "He just loved blueberries, and he was a friendly goat

Weighing in some freshly picked blueberries

Getting a peach display ready at the Fulton Street Farmers' Market

too. He just liked to head-butt a little, just being playful. Suddenly, I saw buckets flying all over the place. And then the family came running out, screaming, 'Help! There's a wild animal loose in there!' City folk are sort of funny sometimes," she concluded.

Having lived in the city for some years, we learned our lesson from Brita's tale, and we keep our cool when we u-pick. It's fun, but it's work, and you may get hot. When we pick berries, we wear broad-brimmed hats and we put sunscreen on the backs of our necks. You should too, because there's little shade out in the fields. Also, consider the time of day. Try to pick in the morning, sometime after the dew is off the fruit but before it's gotten very hot.

And when you're picking fruit from trees, make sure your ladder is on level ground and that somebody in your party knows just where you are, just in case you fall.

Children also love to go picking, and it's fun to take them. Patty and Jim Miller operate a u-pick farm in Coloma, and for five years they've been planting an orchard of "little kid trees," so even the smallest can enjoy picking. This orchard is close to the Miller's Old Barn Market store, where parents can easily stand back and watch the kids without interfering.

The trees in this orchard are unique dwarf trees, imported from Germany, which won't get more than five or six feet tall. Grafted on the German root stock are trees of standard American varieties, so kids picking from the "little kid trees" will harvest the same kind of fruit as their elders.

The Millers also grow a lot of peaches, twelve or thirteen kinds, and by the end of July, some varieties are ready for market. Blueberries are still available then, and nothing is better than peaches and blueberries in cream or with cereal.

Peaches

Jim Miller says that peaches are ripe for picking "when the suture fills out" — that's the line dividing the peach in half. Jim will try and pick those peaches within two days. At the market, look for size and rosy red color. And if it smells like a peach, it's ready to be eaten.

Peaches are a sensitive crop, easily affected by weather. 1992 was a bad year, with just two sunny days in July. But the weather in 1993 was perfect, and peaches worth celebrating were harvested. Red Garnets, which are cling peaches, are among the first to reach market. Red Havens, which are freestone peaches, have the best name recognition and grow well in Michigan. They're our most common peaches and the ones most readily available at our farm markets. But Arnold Groeneveld at the Fulton Street Farmers' Market warns that the early Red Havens "are kind of clingy."

Al Meeusen has been growing two newer varieties of peaches, Belle Aire and Harmony, and recommends both highly. He says that both are a little sweeter than Red Havens.

To freeze peaches, cut them in half, remove the stones, put them in freezer bags, and freeze them flat side down. Mary Bethel Robinette uses Fruit Fresh, according to package directions, to keep the peach flesh from darkening.

The first apples, transparents, also make their appearance toward the end of July. These are fine cooking apples, but a young

Early Apples

woman who tends a farm stand on M-25 east of Bay City warned us about them by puckering up her face and saying, "Transparents are kind of dry and tart. I wouldn't try eating them."

Tomatoes

Early summer is salad time. Through improvements in shipping and storage technology, supermarket tomatoes taste better all the time, but the appearance of vine-ripened, homegrown tomatoes in our farm markets is a blessing worth celebrating. The first to reach market are the homegrown hothouse tomatoes, which Marge Geukes of the Fulton Street market swears are the best-tasting of all tomatoes. Of course, that may just be a response to the long absence of any homegrown tomatoes from the markets, but it's difficult to argue with her about their quality.

Lettuce

Leaf lettuce is the first lettuce to appear at markets, notably Grand Rapids lettuce in huge, circular mounds at the Fulton Street Farmers' Market. It's quickly followed by other green-leaf varieties, red leaf, romaine, Bibb, and Boston lettuce. Mr. Visser at the Fulton Street market says that 1993 was "a tough year for iceberg. The deer got most of my crop."

Since each variety of lettuce has its own taste and texture, we like to mix varieties in our tossed salads. We especially like to combine Bibb, red leaf, and Grand Rapids lettuce.

Peas

Spring peas reach market in Michigan at about the same time as the lettuce. And we suggest that if you cook the peas with some lettuce, as the French do, they'll taste better. It's a good way to freshen up frozen peas too.

Radishes

Red radishes add spice and heat to the salads, although the early summer radishes are not as hot as the midsummer ones. White radishes, also available in early summer, are hotter than the red, and make the best radish sandwiches on buttered rye bread.

We prefer to buy our radishes from the stall run by Mr. Visser. He's a real root farmer, specializing in potatoes and onions, and he has massive amounts of radishes beautifully arranged in two-foot-high spirals.

Carrots

In early summer Mr. Visser and other farmers also sell baby carrots. These are the most tender carrots of the year, and are often used raw in salads.

Green Onions

Green onions, or bunching onions, are all over the market in early summer, and their pervasive smell makes your mouth water as you walk down the aisle. Buy bunches to put in salads,

An artistic tumble of radishes makes a mouthwatering display.

to eat raw as crudités, or to use in cooking, particularly in stir-fried dishes.

Cucumbers, particularly the small green fruits best for pickling, are also available in early summer. There are dozens of ways to make pickles, and each farmer has an old family recipe to share. We're a little leery of passing on these recipes, since we remember when a cookbook was recalled a few years ago because the canning advice was truly volatile: if readers followed the canning advice, they'd blow up their kitchens. And we're even more reluctant after reading the advice of Ann Wells, the food editor of the *Grand Rapids Press*, who wrote, "Those old canning cookbooks and recipes of grandmother's should be kept only for nostalgic reasons. Don't use the recipes. Old-time canning techniques are no longer considered safe, even if you think no one has ever gotten sick from foods canned by those methods. Remember, in the 'olden days' one often didn't know what caused illness."

So, instead of providing recipes, we suggest you learn more about food preservation by taking a correspondence course offered

Cucumbers

by the Oakland County Cooperative Extension Service. Their course is seven weeks long, it's inexpensive (fifteen dollars in 1993), and it details up-to-date, USDA-approved methods of food preservation. For information, write to this address:

Cooperative Extension Service
1200 N. Telegraph Rd., Dept. 416
Pontiac, MI 48341-0416

We will make two small exceptions, though, and include two recipes that cucumber pickle farmers gave us. The first, written on one of those little brown bags that farmers use to package your produce, is a recipe for sour-dill, "kosher" crock pickles. That's the kind of pickle that starred in the movie *Crossing Delancey* — and it's rare when a vegetable gets that kind of billing. The other is for iceberg pickles. We figure that no book about farm markets would be complete without pickle recipes. And Cecile Turner, Home Economist for the Kent County Cooperative Extension Service of Michigan State University, says, "The pickles, including Don's brine pickles, should be O.K. You'll know it when pickles go bad. They'll turn slimy and mushy, and you won't eat them."

Every year we take some of our sour pickles to one of the potlucks at our book discussion club, and those sophisticated readers and eaters gobble them up, none of them dying. It's the only time we share our pickles.

Beans   Beans are also an important part of early summer, and farmers will show mounds of beans — green, wax, and purple. Signs proudly broadcast "First Pickings," and we suppose these are the best, but we buy beans all season long and detect little difference in taste or quality. Farmers do grow a huge variety of beans, so if you do value first pickings, one variety or another always seems to be coming into season, and first pickings are available for a long time.

Each variety of beans will have its own taste and quality. You may thus be faced with a choice of a sweet variety or one that offers unusual tenderness. No need for you to learn which is which. A good farmer like James DeVries, an organic farmer who just loves beans, will present just that choice to you when you ask him which is best. When we pressed him about his favorites,

A sea of beans spills invitingly over a market table.

he told us, "Blue Lakes have good bean flavor, and have been around a long time. They're the only old beans I still grow. My Eagles are real good, too." We often buy beans from Pauline Strick, who after twenty years knows our taste and will say to us, "This is the kind you like." She'll also say, "If you can't decide today, mix the wax and green beans. That makes a real pretty vegetable."

Green beans also freeze well. We process them in half-pound portions, just enough for two generous servings. We cut and trim the beans, blanch them in a wire basket until "the color changes" (usually less than a minute), dunk them in ice water to stop the cooking, dry them on dish towels, and freeze them in plastic bags. And when we use them in winter, they have the taste and consistency of fresh summer beans.

Finally, zucchini shows up on farm stands in mid-July. "And that's quite enough about that!" Don says — although Nelle likes zucchini, and everyone offered us zucchini recipes, so we've included a few here.

EARLY SUMMER RECIPES

Cold Cucumber Soup

MAKES 32 OUNCES, WHICH SHOULD SERVE FOUR TO SIX

This is a favorite of ours in summer, so good we almost inhale it instead of eating it. It's also one of the easiest recipes to remember — you use one of each ingredient.

  1 large cucumber, peeled, seeded, and cut into chunks
  1 green onion, outer leaves removed and cut into chunks
  1 8-ounce container of plain, nonfat yogurt
  1 14-ounce can chicken broth, defatted
  1 tablespoon lemon juice
  1 teaspoon dried dill weed
  1 large dash garlic salt
    salt and pepper to taste

Put everything in a blender and puree. Chill and garnish with more dill weed (fresh, if possible).

Fagiolini verdi in insalata (Green Bean Salad)

MAKES FOUR GENEROUS SERVINGS

Our son-in-law, Simon Klein, lived for a time in Northern Italy. He grew to love Italian food, and now we can always send him the latest Italian cookbook as a present. He's discovered that the best recipes are often the simplest, and he insists that we include this salad, which is served warm.

  1 pound fresh green beans
  1½ tablespoons salt (adjusted to taste)

extra-virgin olive oil
lemon juice

Trim and wash the beans and boil them in salted water until tender. Cooking time will vary with the variety, size, and freshness of the beans. Very young, fresh beans may need to cook only six or seven minutes, while older ones may take ten or twelve.

After cooking, drain the beans and put them in a salad bowl, adding more salt to taste. Then toss the beans with just enough olive oil to give all the beans a thin, glossy coating. Add lemon juice to give the salad a slightly tart taste. Toss again and serve immediately.

Creamy Tarragon Pesto

MAKES TWO CUPS

Ray Kwapil is a retired editor of the Grand Rapids Press *and a dedicated herbalist, raising tarragon and other herbs in a backyard garden. Ray gives us a cup or so of this pesto every year, and we keep it frozen to enjoy on special occasions. It's good stuff.*

¾ cup fresh tarragon
¼ cup fresh parsley
¼ cup walnuts
2 tablespoons cream cheese
3 tablespoons milk
1 tablespoon hot water
1 tablespoon lemon juice
2 tablespoons Romano cheese, grated
½ cup olive oil
   salt and pepper to taste

Mix all the ingredients, except the oil, in a food processor or blender. Slowly add the oil and process until smooth, adding more oil if necessary. Season with salt and pepper to taste. This pesto can be refrigerated for short periods or frozen.

Carrot Salad

SERVES TWO

Ray Kwapil, retired editor, herbalist, and gourmet cook, makes this carrot salad for company.

    3 tablespoons raisins
    3 medium carrots, shredded
 1½ tablespoons onions, finely chopped or minced
    4 tablespoons olive oil
    1 teaspoon vinegar
    1 teaspoon Dijon mustard
    1 teaspoon water
    1 teaspoon sugar
      salt

Place the raisins in a shallow dish or pan, cover with white wine or water, and microwave or heat to just below the boiling point. Set aside to cool and plump for half an hour.

Put the carrots and the onion into a mixing bowl, then add the cooled and drained raisins.

Place the remaining ingredients in a small dish or small mixing bowl and whisk vigorously until thoroughly blended. Add salt and/or more sugar to taste.

Pour this mixture over the carrots, onions, and raisins, and stir together. Store in the refrigerator an hour or more, stirring at least once more, to develop the flavor. Stir again before serving.

Dilled Vegetable Sticks

SERVES FOUR

Deanna House writes in her Even More House Specialties *cookbook: "Raw vegetables are commonplace when we plan appetizers and snacks. For a change of pace, do try these crisply cooked, delicious dilled vegetables. Be prepared; you may be asked for the recipe." And so we asked her if we could share it with you.*

2 cups water
¾ cup vinegar
½ cup sugar
1 teaspoon salt
1½ tablespoons chopped fresh dill weed or 1½ teaspoons dried dill weed
1 teaspoon onion powder
¼ teaspoon garlic powder
½ pound fresh whole green beans, tips removed
3 large carrots, scraped and cut into julienne strips
3 stalks celery, cut into julienne strips

Combine the water, vinegar, sugar, salt, dill weed, onion powder, and garlic powder in a large Dutch oven or saucepan. Bring to a boil, cover, and simmer for fifteen minutes. Then add the beans, carrots, and celery. Return the mixture to a boil, cover, and simmer for five minutes, or until the vegetables are crisp-tender. Put the vegetables along with the vinegar mixture in a shallow container and chill for at least eight hours. Drain before serving.

Icicle Pickles

Leona Van Koevering has been selling us cucumbers and dill for pickles at the Fulton Street Farmers' Market for over twenty years. She's a hale and hearty farmer who just loves her icicle pickles and has told us how good they are every one of those twenty-odd years. So we had to include her recipe.

1 gallon water
2 cups canning salt
2 gallons pickles, cut in strips
1 gallon water
1 lump alum

SYRUP:
8 pints sugar
2½ quarts yellow vinegar
1 handful mixed pickling spices

Dissolve the canning salt in a gallon of water and bring to a boil. Pour over the pickles and let stand in a crock or nonreactive container, covered, for a week. Drain, then dissolve the alum in a gallon of water and pour over the pickles. The next day, rinse the pickles with a gallon of clear water and drain. Combine the ingredients for the syrup, bring to a boil, and pour over the pickles. Repeat the rinsing and "syruping" procedure for four or five mornings, and then seal the pickles in jars.

Authors' note: Pickles may go bad and shouldn't be eaten then. Try storing them in the refrigerator for longer shelf life.

Don's Pickles

One day, about twenty years ago, I saw some lovely looking cucumbers at the Fulton Street Farmers' Market, and I remarked that I hadn't had a great pickle since leaving New York. The old farmer tending that stall heard me and suggested that I make my own. When that seemed farfetched to me, she explained that it was simple, that anybody could make pickles, and scrawled this recipe on the back of a brown paper bag: 12 quarts water, 2 cups salt (coarse), 2 cups vinegar. Boil. When cool, pour over pickles.

A customer standing there added that, if I wanted them New York style, I would have to add a lot of garlic. He wrote his name, Ted, and his phone number on a piece of paper from his pocket notebook and said I could call him for advice if I needed more.

The farmer chimed in again and said that if I really wanted great pickles, I would have to use fresh pickling spices — and her dill. I was armed and ready, so I bought the cucumbers and dill, stopped at the hardware store and bought a colorful crock, stopped at the supermarket and bought the coarse salt and a brand new jar of pickling spices, and made my pickles. They were terrible. But I had the crock, and I bought a book on pickling and kept trying, and now my pickles rival those of New York. Surprisingly, the book told me to do just what my farmer and Ted had suggested. Some batches, I think, just don't work. We have since switched from the old crock to a plastic food container, and the pickles seem to do better.

```
        2  gallons water
     1½  cups coarse salt, not iodized
        2  cups distilled white vinegar (5 percent acidity)
    40-50  cucumbers, 5-6 inches long
           fresh dill
        ¾  cup fresh whole mixed pickling spices
     6-10  garlic cloves, diced
```

Dissolve the salt in the water and bring to a rapid boil. Add the vinegar and reboil, then cover and let cool. While the brine is cooling, wash the pickles, using a stiff-bristled vegetable brush, and discard any that feel soft or are bruised. (It's important to get all the mud off, but you want to be gentle to avoid injuring the skins.)

Arrange some dill, a little of the pickling spices, and some of the garlic in a layer at the bottom of the crock, and cover with a layer of pickles packed tightly. Cover with another layer of spices, and repeat the process until all the pickles are in the crock. Cover the last layer with a heavy plate to hold the pickles down and pour on the brine. Then close the crock, opening it at least once a day to check the pickles.

A scum will form, and it should be skimmed off daily. Any pickles that come in contact with the scum will be ruined, so make sure they keep well below the surface, adding more brine if necessary.

In about three weeks, the brine will be quite cloudy, and the pickles will be ready to taste. If they're good, make some fresh brine, and while it's still hot, pour it over some rinsed pickles in a clean jar. Let them cool awhile, then refrigerate. Eat these first, and when they're gone, make another jarful from those left in the crock. They'll be softer than the first batch, and a bit more sour.

Authors' note: It is most important to use the proportions of salt and water indicated. Too weak a brine, and the pickles will spoil. Too strong, and they will shrivel. And please remember that coarse salt is specified, and a cup of that salt may be half what a cup of table salt would be.

Italian Coleslaw

SERVES TWO

We're not sure just how Italian this recipe is, but that's what they call it at Charley's Crab. Ours is inspired by theirs, and ours also reminds us of a romantic day that we were served a wonderful cabbage salad on a train speeding through the middle of France. The French coleslaw wasn't peppery.

- 1 tablespoon extra-virgin olive oil
- 1 tablespoon balsamic vinegar
- ¼ teaspoon dry mustard or ½ teaspoon prepared Dijon mustard
- dash ground cayenne pepper
- salt to taste
- ½ teaspoon celery seed
- ¼ head cabbage, shredded, or enough for two (a mix of red and green is pretty)
- 2 green onions, sliced in thin rings
- 1 small carrot, shredded
- ½ small green pepper, cut into thin strips

Whisk together the first six ingredients, add the vegetables, and toss well. Let the vegetables stand thirty minutes to an hour to allow the flavors to blend, and toss again before serving. This can be served chilled or at room temperature.

Authors' note: Both natural and prepared products differ in strength, notably mustard, balsamic vinegar, and cayenne pepper. Particularly with the latter, we have to experiment with each new batch. Until you know how hot your pepper is, it's best to start light. You can always add more before serving. Similarly, the strength of Dijon mustard varies widely with the brand.

Great Green·Beans

SERVES FOUR

Deanna House is a busy, bustling woman who always seems to be off to an appointment or on some important errand. She's also a home economist and a fine cook who fortunately has discovered the time-saving virtues of microwave cooking. Now she's authored three cookbooks, and in most of the recipes she offers directions for the microwave oven. This recipe is from Even More House Specialties. *She writes, "Here is a great way to show off fresh green beans. It really is worth a trip to the garden or your favorite farmer's market just to find fresh beans for this recipe. However, when necessary, frozen green beans are a good substitute."*

- ½ cup water
- 3 cups fresh green beans, washed and trimmed (about one pound) or 3 cups frozen
- ½ cup green onions, sliced
- 1 cup fresh mushrooms, sliced
- 2 tablespoons margarine
- salt and pepper to taste

In a 2-quart, microwave-safe casserole, combine the water and beans. Cover with a lid or vented plastic wrap. Microwave on full power for 7 to 9 minutes, or until the beans are crisp-tender, stirring once. Let stand one minute, then drain.

In a 1-quart, microwave-safe bowl, combine the onions, mushrooms, and margarine. Microwave on full power for 2 to 3 minutes, or until the onions are crisp-tender.

Stir the onions and mushrooms into the drained beans, and season to taste with salt and pepper. Microwave at full power for 2 to 3 minutes until hot, stirring once.

Grilled Lake Michigan Whitefish

SERVES TWO

We first saw this recipe posted on the wall at Carlson's Fish Market in Leland's Fishtown. We made it that night, and do so at least three or four times each summer. When we asked permission to share this recipe with you, Bill Carlson said, "You know, that's really good. We haven't done that in a long time, but I think we'll have it tonight."

    1 large tomato
    1 medium onion
    1 green pepper
    ½ fresh lemon
    6-8 fresh mushrooms
    2 whitefish fillets, ½ to ¾ pound each
    2 tablespoons butter or margarine
    ¼ cup Good Harbor Birch White wine
      salt and pepper to taste

Slice the tomato, onion, green pepper, and lemon in ¼-inch rounds. Slice the mushrooms in ¼-inch–thick slices. Butter a square of heavy-duty aluminum foil and place one of the fillets skin side down in the center. Turn up the edges of the foil to form a pan. Arrange the sliced vegetables and lemon on the fillet, covering it completely. Dot with butter, then add the wine, salt, and pepper (and any herbs you might like). Cover with the second fillet, skin side up.

   Fold the foil over and seal it tightly. Grill for ten minutes over hot coals, then turn the packet, being careful not to puncture the foil, and grill another ten minutes.

Authors' note: This is a recipe that's fun to play with. Add herbs like oregano and thyme, or throw in other vegetables like zucchini.

No-Bake Red Tart Cherry Pie

MAKES TWO PIES

Herb and Liz Teichman, the owners of Tree-Mendus Fruit in Eau Claire, have published a number of cookbooks that may be purchased at their farm. Liz has graciously allowed us to share with you this recipe from their Tree-Mendus Farm Family Recipes & Collections.

- 2 tablespoons cornstarch
- 1½ cups water
- ¾ cup sugar
- 6 ounces cherry Jell-O mix
- 1 quart red tart cherries, pitted and chopped
- 1 package Dream Whip, whipped

Mix the cornstarch, water, and sugar, and bring to a boil over low heat. Boil the mixture about two minutes, or until it clears. Add the cherry Jell-O, stirring until it dissolves. Remove from heat, then add the cherries. When the mixture starts to set, blend in the Dream Whip. Pour into two 8-inch baked pie shells.

Raspberry Pie

MAKES TWO PIES

Sometime in early summer, Diane Platte of the Platte Family Farm brings her first picking of raspberries to the Fulton Street Farmers' Market. It's an exciting moment. The first crop doesn't last long, and soon Diane is bringing in her corn and apples, but in late summer and through the fall she brings her second crop of raspberries, and it's again an exciting time. This is her old family recipe for raspberry pie.

CRUST:
- 2 cups flour
- ¾ cup shortening
- 1 teaspoon salt

⅓ cup water, more or less, to make the dough a
  good consistency

Mix all ingredients until the dough forms a ball. Then divide the dough in half and roll out both halves. Divide one of the halves and line two 8- or 9-inch pie plates.

> FILLING:
> 1 quart raspberries
> 3 tablespoons Minute tapioca
> ¾ cup sugar

Mix the ingredients together thoroughly, then fill the two prepared pie plates. Divide the remaining half of the dough into two pieces and put a top on each pie. Cut a few slits in each top crust to allow steam to escape. Bake at 425° for 10 minutes, then turn down to 350° and bake for another 50 minutes.

Blueberry Buckle

SERVES NINE

We stopped to chat with Diane Platte at the Fulton Street Farmers' Market on the day she first brought her marvelous raspberries to market. We asked her for a recipe, and she talked enthusiastically about her raspberry pie. But Stacy Platte, her daughter, interrupted with "Mom, what about the blueberry buckle? That's really good."

And then Rachel Platte chimed in: "Blueberry buckle is the best dessert ever." So we had to have this recipe, too.

> BATTER:
> ¾ cup sugar
> ¼ cup margarine
> 1 egg
> 2 cups flour
> 2 teaspoons baking powder
> ½ teaspoon salt

½ cup milk
2 cups blueberries, fresh or home-frozen

CRUMB TOPPING:
½ cup sugar
⅓ cup flour
½ teaspoon ground cinnamon
¼ cup firm margarine

In a large bowl, mix the sugar, margarine, and egg until creamy. Sift the flour, baking powder, and salt together in a small bowl. Alternately add small amounts of the flour mixture and the milk to the egg mixture. Beat until smooth, then gently stir in the blueberries.

To make the topping, combine the dry ingredients and cut in the margarine to make a crumbly mixture. Spread the batter in a greased and floured 9 × 13-inch pan, and sprinkle the topping over the batter. Bake at 375° for 30 minutes.

Blueberry Muffins

MAKES 18 MUFFINS

We picked up this recipe at the Blueberry Festival in South Haven, published in a brochure titled "Blueberries: Traditional Recipes," which is distributed by the Michigan Blueberry Growers. If you'd like a copy, write to MBG Marketing, P.O. Drawer B, Grand Junction, MI 49056.

2 cups flour
2 teaspoons baking powder
1 teaspoon ground cinnamon
¼ teaspoon salt
2 eggs
1 cup milk
¾ cup sugar
½ cup vegetable oil
1 cup blueberries, fresh or frozen

Combine the flour, baking powder, cinnamon, and salt. Mix well. Beat the eggs lightly, and stir in the milk, sugar, and oil. Quickly stir this egg mixture into the dry ingredients, and then carefully stir in the blueberries. Spoon the batter into a greased muffin pan and bake at 400° for 15 to 17 minutes.

Authors' note: The proportions in this recipe make marvelous muffins, but the way we fill our muffin cups, we can never stretch the batter to make eighteen.

Blueberry Sauce

MAKES ABOUT TWO CUPS

This recipe also comes from "Blueberries: Traditional Recipes," published by the Michigan Blueberry Growers.

> 2 cups blueberries, fresh or frozen
> ¼ cup orange juice
> ¼ cup water
> 2 tablespoons sugar
> 1 tablespoon cornstarch
> ¼ teaspoon grated orange peel
> ⅛ teaspoon ground nutmeg
> dash salt

Combine all ingredients in a saucepan. Cook and stir over medium heat for 4 to 5 minutes, until thickened. Serve on pancakes or waffles, blintzes, ice cream, pudding, or pound cake.

Authors' note: To make a lowfat dessert for a potluck party, we served this sauce over angel-food cake and frozen vanilla yogurt.

Blueberry Cheesecake

SERVES EIGHT

This recipe comes from the kitchen of Brita Soper of the Blueberry Patch in Sawyer, Michigan. This farm publishes a newsletter that advises customers about crop conditions, attractions in the area, and scheduled events. Each issue includes a recipe or two, most very healthy. This cheesecake recipe comes directly from Brita, and is clearly off our diet, but it's too good not to include.

CRUST:
¾ cup flour
1½ tablespoons sugar
6 tablespoons margarine
¼ cup walnuts, chopped

Mix all ingredients together, press into a pie dish, and bake for 10 minutes at 375°. Cool thoroughly.

FILLING:
1 8-ounce package softened cream cheese
2 eggs
¾ cup sugar
1¼ cup sour cream
¼ teaspoon almond extract

Mix all ingredients and pour into the cooled crust. Bake 30 to 35 minutes at 375°.

TOPPING:
2 cups blueberries
½ cup water
¾ cup sugar
2 tablespoons cornstarch
1 tablespoon lemon juice

Cook these ingredients until thickened, then pour over the top of the pie. You don't need to cool the pie before topping it with the fruit.

Brita tops her blueberry cheesecake with whipped cream. She uses two small containers of whipping cream, 3 heaping tablespoons of powdered sugar, and a teaspoon of vanilla, all beaten together. Might as well go for broke.

SUMMER

IT'S HOT. IT TAKES AN EFFORT TO DO ANYTHING. IT'S THE
lazy time. It's the time when farmers at the market call across the
aisle, "Hey! Turn on the air conditioner." In August, that may be
as far as humor goes.

The greens of the market are cool, from the deep greens of

This farm stand offers a free taste test of its juicy watermelons.

broccoli and peppers to the pale greens of cabbage and lettuce, but the hot colors are the dominant colors in summer, with the blazing yellow sun reflected in the yellowing grain, yellow summer squash, and yellow corn, and in the hot orange-reds of peaches and the deeper reds of apples. The fruits of summer, however, are wet and refreshing. Peaches and plums, juicy apples, and melons — sweet, refreshing cantaloupes and sweeter, wetter watermelons.

Melons

For twenty years, we've asked John Geukes at the Fulton Street Farmers' Market to pick our melons for us. We'll say we need one ready to eat in two days, and John will nod, pass a magical hand over two or three melons, pick one up, and say, "This one will do you. Just leave it on the counter, and it'll be perfect." And he'll be right.

Jeff Dykstra, also at the Fulton Street market, takes some of the magic out of choosing cantaloupes. First, he suggests, squeeze the melon. The firmer it is, the longer it will keep. Next, look at the "stem slip." If it's smooth and veined, the melon has slipped off the vine. If the stem has been cut or yanked off, the farmer has picked the melon early, rather than when ripe. Then smell the melon. If it smells good, it will taste good.

The traditional way to tell if a melon is ripe is to poke the stem-slip end. That's a little bit of a problem, because not-quite-ready melons may give after repeated pokings, while ripe melons puncture easily. Yellow color once reliably indicated a melon was ready, but Jeff says that now some good varieties of melons never fully yellow.

Jeff is also expert at finding good, ripe watermelons. He looks for heavy melons and "thumps" them with the back of his large fruit knife. The hollower the sound, the less ripe the melon. A really ripe melon has a dull sound when thumped.

Peaches

Freestone peaches are readily available in summer, and farmers offer bushel baskets of Red Havens. When fully ripe, they're juicy and sweet, and are good candidates for freezing or canning.

Apples

The early August apples are, by and large, still cooking apples, usually a touch too tart for most people to enjoy as eating apples. An exception: the relatively rare alamato apple, which looks like a tiny red Delicious, is a good eating apple.

In August, the farmers never take a day off — they're too busy picking the harvest: broccoli, cauliflower, cabbage, celery,

The sign describing these cantaloupes says it all.

beans, turnips, potatoes, eggplants, peppers, cucumbers, lettuce, radishes, onions, summer squash, zucchini, spinach, herbs, and corn, corn, corn. Summer is corn-on-the-cob time.

Corn

Norma Andre of Flowers of the Field uses corn in the "farm dinner" she makes for all the pickers. She first bakes a couple of open-face, fresh blackberry pies for dessert. Then she goes to work on the main meal. She cooks up pork chops on an outside grill. (She and her family raise hogs on their farm, so these are "home-grown" pork chops.) She takes freshly dug new red potatoes, boils them, and then tosses them with parsley. She makes coleslaw by mixing chopped cabbage with chopped onions and red, green, and yellow peppers. She puts a big pot of water on to boil and then tells one of her sons, Martin or Peter, to go pick the corn. That's the way corn should be eaten, we are told.

But few of us are able to experience that fresh-from-the-field thrill. The next-best thing is corn picked that morning and put out on the farm stand or brought to the municipal farm market.

Most of the farmers will peel back the husks so customers can see the color and size of kernels and know that there are no corn borers. Farmers get tired of hearing customers scream, "Oooh — there's a worm!" so it's good that they peel some. But corn will keep better in the unpeeled husks. Roasting corn in the husks is a flavorful way of preparing it (first soak the ears thoroughly in some brine), and that requires intact husks. You can even boil corn in the husks, then take each ear, cut off the stem end, and with one pull on the silk end, remove the entire husk and all the silk. That's the way they do it in Maine at lobster shacks. And Marge Geukes offers a tip for microwaving corn: leave two or three layers of husk on the ear and run the oven on high for two or three minutes.

If you choose to buy corn still in the husk and aren't afraid of worms, Betty Nitz suggests how to select it: "You run your hands up and down the ears first, and they should feel filled. Look at the silk, too. It should be dark brown when the corn is ready."

Baskets of corn wait for their turn on the market table.

And it's fun to make corn-husk dolls out of the husks you bring home. Every Brownie Scout knows how to do this, so just find one and get her to show you how.

The proper way to eat corn is a matter of some dispute. It is always proper to butter and salt an ear, pick it up, and chew off the kernels, although some folk still insist on cutting the kernels off the cob and eating the corn daintily with a fork. The real controversy comes in when discussing how to eat it off the ear. Does one start at the fat end, the skinny end, or in the middle? Is it better to eat down the rows, or is it better to eat off a circle of kernels? We choose not to enter the dispute.

Marge Geukes, a mother as well as a farmer, has learned that corn on the cob may be a problem for "kids with front teeth missing or wearing braces." So she slides a sharp knife down the center of the kernels, leaving the tough base of the kernel behind. "This is good for older people with digestive problems, too," she points out.

Corn can be frozen on the cob by cooking it for a few minutes, plunging it in ice water, then drying the ears and packaging them in plastic bags before putting them in the freezer. But most farmers, when asked, say they prefer to freeze cooked kernels. There are slight variations in the methods; in the recipes that follow we've included two that are most commonly suggested.

Broccoli comes to market in a rush, and every farmer has it. Presidential politics and taste aside, it's popular. "Even kids love broccoli now," says Jane Nyenbrink of B.J.'s Farm. "They come and ask for 'the little trees,' and eat them raw. It never used to be that way, and I've been coming to market for twenty years. My own kids never felt that way."

Broccoli

Broccoli has been getting marvelous press, and in the minds of some it's now a magic bullet for the cure of all sorts of heinous diseases. But be like the kids — eat it because it tastes good. Buy the little trees to dunk raw or parboiled in dips. Steam or boil broccoli to serve as a side dish, and try squeezing some lemon juice on it. Or serve it with a creamy cheese sauce.

And cheese-broccoli soup has become the restaurant rage in Michigan, and can be easily mimicked at home. But you probably can't serve that soup as health food — it's got too much fat in it.

Broccoli is often served mixed with cauliflower, and that makes an unusually pretty vegetable dish.

Cauliflower

Like broccoli florets, cauliflower florets are nice for dipping. And like broccoli, cauliflower is steamed or boiled to serve as a side dish. Often it's topped with a bread-crumb butter mixture or a cheese sauce.

Both broccoli and cauliflower are members of the cabbage family, and cabbage comes into its own in the summer. We like to shred both green and red cabbage and use it in our tossed salads.

Cabbage

Cabbage can also be used to make a variety of slaws. A mayonnaise-based dressing makes coleslaw; a sweet-and-sour vinegar dressing makes garden slaw. The French make a "cole-slaw" with a simple oil-and-vinegar dressing, and Charley's Crab makes a wonderful, spicy "Italian coleslaw." We like it so much that we've tried to imitate it at home, and we've included our recipe here (with the spring recipes). Charley's is better, but ours is close.

Celery

Celery, onions, and peppers add crunch and spice to salads and other dishes. Cooks in New Orleans call a mixture of the three "the Trinity," and they use it in everything from gumbo to étouffée to jambalaya. Gert Eding, a celery specialist who sells at the Holland Municipal Farm Market, says that she "adds lots of celery to anything I cook," and suggests that you "cut up equal portions of celery, peppers, and onions, and freeze them all together in one-cup portions." That way you can have the taste of summer in your soups all winter.

Gert starts her vegetables in the greenhouse in February, but she grows more than just the "Hudsonville" celery. (The town of Hudsonville smells like celery for much of the summer.) She also grows bok choy and celery cabbage, and reports that she has good customer response to these Chinese vegetables.

Farmers also grow a variety of peppers, with one farmer bragging that he now harvests twenty-eight kinds. Pick bell peppers that are unbruised, smooth skinned, and feel heavy. The old green bell pepper is still the basic pepper, but now you can get red (actually a fully ripe green bell pepper), yellow, and purple peppers. When asked to describe the taste of these new purple peppers, that same pepper farmer said, "They taste just like the green ones." That may not be quite true, but it's close. There is more difference in texture — red peppers, for example, are notably softer than green. But if you cut up and combine the different

A dazzling array of summer vegetables at Eastern Market

peppers, you have a wonderfully colorful and attractive vegetable dish. (Serve blue peppers alone, and see if anybody guesses right off what they are. Taste, evidently, is partly visual.)

Hot peppers are another story. The hot red peppers give warning by their color, but mild-looking banana peppers can also

*Sweet peppers, leeks, and onions on display
at the Grand Haven farm market*

take the roof off your mouth. And if you're going to prepare jalapeno peppers for cooking, wear gloves and be sure you don't wipe your eyes and face with your hands. Nothing burns worse.

Tomatoes   Fresh tomatoes are a major feature at summer farm markets, with farmers displaying baskets of cherry tomatoes and five-inch beefsteak tomatoes, big enough for one center slice to cover the largest hamburger you might grill. Beefsteak is still our favorite, perhaps because its name invokes a forbidden fruit to cholesterol watchers like us, but it seems that new varieties come to market every year. Of the now-standard types, both Jet Star and Super Sonics have great tomato taste.

Farmers will tell you that the best way to eat tomatoes is at room temperature, with a little salt and pepper. Chilling tends to reduce flavor. We like to slice tomatoes and splash them with oil and vinegar seasoned with fresh dill weed (which also reaches market in midsummer). And we serve sliced tomatoes, in one form or another, all summer, frequently combined with whatever fresh herbs are available.

We chatted with Nancy Bruursema about tomatoes. She and her husband, Scott, own Radseck's Farm Market on the Blue Star Highway south of Saugatuck. It's one of the most interesting farm stands. Scott's grandfather started the farm, and Nancy and Scott display what they grow in antique baskets, baby buggies, and recycled store fixtures. It's a friendly place, and Scott will offer to show you his chickens as well as sell you produce.

We happened to be there at the peak of their tomato harvest, so we asked Nancy how she served them. She too likes them best when they're sliced and flavored with fresh herbs, but she also said that just that day she had served them with fresh basil stirred into mayonnaise.

Eggplant is a summer vegetable that cooks usually flavor *Eggplant* heavily with herbs and spices. To tell if an eggplant is ripe, gently

Beefsteak tomatoes like these remain our personal favorites.

press on it with your thumb. If it gives but bounces back, it's ripe. If the dent stays, the eggplant is overripe. If the eggplant doesn't yield to gentle pressure, it's underripe. Gentle pressure is the key. At the Royal Oak Market, we listened to one farmer who had bushel baskets filled with lavender eggplants say repeatedly, "Hey, lady. Don't bruise my eggplants." His were beautiful, and he was right to be sensitive.

Now, if you've ever wondered why eggplant is called that, we might have found the answer. Susan Brennan Barnes and Lilli Congdon, of East Branch Specialty Farms, brought some small white eggplants to Kalamazoo's Bank Street Market. They looked just like eggs wearing green elfin caps.

To make a fine appetizer, take an eggplant and slice it, salt the slices (eggplant is very wet and tends to get mushy unless you draw out the water with salt or press the slices like cucumber slices), and sauté them in oil with garlic and herbs. Be careful — eggplant soaks up oil like a sponge. Combining eggplant with other vegetables to make ratatouille is also a good way to use this vegetable — we've included a recipe here.

Potatoes

Michigan potatoes are another mainstay of summer markets. Small new potatoes, white and red, are the most common, with russets coming later in the fall. For the best taste, boil them and toss them in a little butter with parsley, dill, or rosemary. They need not be peeled, but for a nice presentation, try removing one strip of peel around the middle of each potato.

We also like to roast potato slices coated with a minimal amount of olive oil and dusted with some fresh herbs. These "potato chips" are better for you than the standard variety, albeit not as crisp.

Summer Squash

Summer squash, straight neck or crookneck, is a delicate summer vegetable. It has a thin skin and need not be peeled for cooking. Steaming, boiling, and sautéing are all good methods of preparation. It takes only three or four minutes to sauté diced or sliced summer squash in butter or olive oil, so it's great when you don't want to spend much time in the kitchen. You also don't need to sauce or spice summer squash. Just add salt and pepper to taste. Most often, sauces will only overpower this vegetable's delicate taste.

Zucchini is another matter. Zucchini can also be sautéed, but

The season's bounty: a basket brimming over with summer squash

frequently cooks will add spiced tomato sauce, garlic, onions, other strong-flavored vegetables, and strong cheese — aged, grated Parmesan, for example. "Something's got to overpower the zucchini," says Don.

So it's nice that increasing numbers of farmers grow herbs for market. Betty Nitz and the organic farmers, Chaz Bauer and James DeVries, have huge bunches of basil for sale throughout the summer. We love the taste of fresh basil leaves. We like to slice them in strips and serve them on tomato slices topped with fresh mozzarella cheese and dressed with a little olive oil and balsamic vinegar. Despite the simplicity of this dish, it's the most popular summer appetizer served in the upscale Italian sidewalk cafés in New York and Boston.

Herbs may be used fresh or dried for year-round use. Flowers

Herbs

of the Field in Grand Rapids even sells some dried herbs, including a beautiful oregano, as dried flowers.

Most people use herbs in combination. You can make a variety of sauces by stewing some fresh tomatoes in various combinations of herbs and adding some celery, peppers, and onions. Basil, oregano, and garlic yield an Italian taste, oregano a Greek taste, and garlic and thyme a Provençal taste. We bought a "Simon & Garfunkel" bunch of herbs from the Frog Holler Organic Farmers at the Kerrytown Market in Ann Arbor. As you might suspect, it's a mix of parsley, sage, rosemary, and thyme, and they suggest you chop it, sauté it in olive oil, and add it to vegetables or soup for a "robust flavor." That works, except we eliminate the sage, which reminds us too much of turkey stuffing.

Every year, Ray Kwapil, a retired editor at the *Grand Rapids Press,* presents us with a large bottle of his tarragon vinegar and a cup (frozen) of his tarragon pesto sauce, both labeled "From the Garden of Ray Kwapil, Herbalist." We hoard these and use them all year. Herb-flavored vinegars are a fine way to use herbs. Commercial growers produce a variety of herb vinegars, and some of the best we've tasted are made by Pat Bourdo of Woodland Herb Farm in Northport. For a treat, you can simply dip some bread in Pat's vinegars — they're that smooth and tasty. Pat also makes fruit and wine vinegars; our favorite is her "Verry Cherry Wine Vinegar."

Pat and others cautioned us against storing herb- and garlic-flavored oils, the kind you see served in Italian restaurants for bread dipping — and they're right. These oils are wonderful, and they lower the amount of saturated fat in your diet when you substitute them for butter. But Cecille Turner of the Kent County Extension Service of Michigan State University warns of the dangers. In an article printed on 15 August 1993 in the *Grand Rapids Press,* she recounted the story of the lady who called to ask what was growing on the herbs in her olive oil. It turned out that she was growing bacteria that produced the deadly toxin which causes botulism. Ms. Turner went on to issue these cautions:

> A few years ago, the Food and Drug Administration (FDA) issued a warning about putting garlic in oil and storing the mixture at room temperature. The same principle applies to putting herbs in oil. It is not safe.

Because of the risk of botulism poisoning, the FDA has ordered food processing companies to stop making any garlic-in-oil mixes that must be refrigerated.

. . . To be safe, . . . products must contain specific levels of microorganism inhibitors or acidifying agents. . . . Most garlic or herb products contain these additives, as disclosed on their labels, but some boutiques or specialty mixes may not have included these additives.

So if you want to use herb- or garlic-flavored oils, for safety's sake read the label carefully before you buy a commercial preparation. If you want to prepare these oils at home, use them only when they're fresh, and don't try to store them.

SUMMER RECIPES

Chicken or Turkey Gumbo

SERVES FOUR TO SIX

Okra is one of the minor vegetables at farm markets, and it only appears for a moment in time, but when you see it, you should take advantage of this or another recipe and make a big pot of gumbo.

- ¼ cup vegetable oil
- ⅓ cup flour
- 1 medium onion, diced
- ½ large green pepper, diced
- 3 ribs celery, diced
- 2 cloves garlic, minced
- 2½ cups chicken broth
- 2 cups stewed tomatoes
- ⅔ pound raw chicken breast or turkey tenderloin, diced in ½-inch cubes
- ¼ teaspoon cayenne pepper
- 1 teaspoon Tabasco sauce
- 1 teaspoon dried thyme
- 1 tablespoon Worcestershire sauce
- 1 tablespoon lemon juice
- 1 cup cooked rice (or equivalent dry rice and water)
- 2 cups fresh okra, sliced (or one cup frozen)
  salt and pepper to taste

Make a roux by sautéing the oil and flour until they're a caramel brown. In that roux, sauté the onion, green pepper, celery, and garlic. Transfer the mixture to a large stockpot and add the chicken broth, stewed tomatoes, chicken, cayenne pepper, Tabasco sauce, thyme, Worcestershire sauce, and lemon juice. Bring to a boil and simmer until slightly thickened. (Gumbo is a thick soup, but if you like it thinner, you can add more broth or water.)

About half an hour before serving, add the rice. About ten minutes before serving, add the okra. Along with that, you can add a half-pound of peeled, deveined shrimp, or some spicy cooked sausage.

Authors' note: Make sure you have a bottle of Tabasco sauce on the table when you serve this. Some people prefer gumbo really hot.

Cold Italian Eggplant Salad

SERVES THREE TO FOUR

One day when we visited the Holland Municipal Farm Market, we found Bob Kettlehake, Executive Sous-Chef for Premiere Food Service at Haworth Corporation. He was testing eggplants for ripeness, and we asked him what he planned to do with them. What he told us sounded so good, we asked him to let us share his recipe.

  1 medium eggplant, sliced in ¼-inch rounds
  ¼ cup seasoned flour (salt, pepper, paprika,
       and Italian herbs to taste)
  ¼ cup seasoned bread crumbs (Italian preferred)
  2 tablespoons olive oil
  2 cloves garlic
  ½ medium purple onion, sliced in thin rounds
3-4 Roma tomatoes, seeded and coarsely chopped
  1 lemon, seeded and coarsely chopped
  2 tablespoons olive oil
     fresh basil leaves

Pat the eggplant slices dry and dredge with the seasoned flour. Pat on the seasoned bread crumbs. Sauté the garlic cloves in olive oil until golden brown, then fish out the garlic and discard. Add the breaded eggplant slices to the garlic-infused oil and sauté until golden brown, being careful not to scorch them.

    Arrange the slices on a plate or platter, starting in the center and working to the outer edge, lightly overlapping pieces. Then spread the onion rings, chopped tomatoes, and lemon pieces over the eggplant, and drizzle fresh olive oil over the whole mix.

Strategically place the basil around the platter both for garnish and for flavor, to be eaten as part of the dish.

Let the dish stand a few hours before serving. Or let it marinate overnight in the refrigerator and serve it cold as a salad.

Scalloped Celery

SERVES THREE

Ray Kwapil, our favorite herbalist, suggests this unusual use for one of West Michigan's most widely grown vegetables. Savory adds a special flavor.

2 cups celery, sliced
¼ teaspoon salt
½ teaspoon savory
1 tablespoon onion or chives, finely chopped
2 tablespoons flour
¼ cup chicken broth or bouillon
½ cup milk
¼ teaspoon ground pepper
¾ cup Velveeta or cheddar cheese, shredded
2 tablespoons butter
½ cup bread crumbs

Place the celery in a saucepan (no water) with the salt. Cover tightly and cook slowly over low heat, shaking the pan occasionally to prevent scorching. When the celery is slightly tender, add the savory and onions, and cook slowly until tender. Add water only if the celery becomes dry. Blend in the flour, then add the broth, milk, and pepper. Stir and bring to a slow boil. Add the cheese and stir until all of it is melted.

Turn out into a small greased casserole or baking dish. Melt the butter, stir the bread crumbs into it, and sprinkle over the top of the casserole. Heat the dish in a moderate oven (375°) or put it under the broiler until the crumbs are browned.

Argiero's Pepperonata Piccante

SERVES FOUR TO SIX

Argiero's Restaurant is across the street from the Kerrytown Market in Ann Arbor. We first visited it with our son-in-law, who had fallen in love with the restaurant as a University of Michigan student and had to introduce it to us. We in turn fell in love with this dish, and Rosa Argiero let us copy the recipe that was posted on the wall. We've been making it for years, but it's still better at Argiero's.

    6 ounces olive oil
    7 medium potatoes, sliced
    5 cayenne peppers, finely chopped
    1 large onion, chopped
    7 green peppers, cut in large chunks
    3 cups fresh tomatoes, peeled and chopped

Sauté the potatoes, cayenne peppers, and onions in olive oil for 10 minutes. Then add the green peppers and tomatoes and cook for another 15 minutes. Serve with good crusty bread, or serve over bread for an open-faced sandwich.

Authors' note: This recipe may be varied considerably. On our last visit to Argiero's, this dish also had banana peppers and zucchini in it. Rosa explained that they were in season, and she had picked some up at the farmers' market.

Greek-Style Vegetable Pasta

SERVES THREE TO FOUR

We first had this dish at Boone's, a seafood restaurant on the wharf in Portland, Maine. We've been playing with the ingredients ever since, and there's nothing that can go wrong. Each time it might taste a little different, but each time it will be delicious. We added zucchini just the last time we made it.

    1 tablespoon olive oil

        1 medium onion, cut in thin wedges
        1 red-green pepper, sliced in thin strips
        3 garlic cloves, minced
        1 small zucchini, sliced
        4 Roma tomatoes, cut in wedges
        2 tablespoons chopped fresh oregano or 1 teaspoon dried
          oregano
        ¼ cup Calamata olives
        8 ounces dry linguine or rotini
        ¼ pound feta cheese, broken into chunks

Heat the olive oil in a nonstick skillet and sauté the vegetables, stirring frequently. Start with the onion and pepper, and when they start to soften, add the garlic and zucchini. When the zucchini begins to soften, add the tomatoes, oregano, and olives.

Cook the pasta as directed, starting while the zucchini is cooking. Drain the pasta — don't rinse it — and toss the vegetables with the pasta in a shallow bowl. Right before serving, add the chunks of feta, and toss again at the table.

Moroccan-Style Vegetables with Couscous

SERVES FOUR

This is a wonderful main-dish recipe for a late-summer dinner. But we always increase this recipe and make enough for leftovers, to serve as a side dish with grilled lamb chops or a plain broiled steak.

        2 tablespoons vegetable oil
        1 medium onion, sliced thin (we often use half a
          red onion and half a yellow)
        ½ green pepper, cut into thin strips
        ½ red pepper, cut into thin strips
        1 teaspoon cinnamon
        2 teaspoons cumin
        ¼ teaspoon cayenne pepper
        1 16-ounce can sliced, stewed tomatoes

(or 14½-ounce can stewed tomatoes)
4-5 small potatoes, peeled and sliced into ¼-inch rounds
  2 tablespoons fresh lime juice
  2 cups broccoli florets
  1 15-ounce can garbanzo beans, drained and rinsed
    salt to taste
  1 package couscous

In a heavy enamel pot, heat the oil and add the onion, peppers, cinnamon, cumin, and cayenne. Cook until the vegetables are soft, about five minutes. Add the tomatoes, potatoes, and lime juice. Cover and simmer twenty minutes until the potatoes are almost done. Then stir in the broccoli and garbanzo beans, bring to a boil, and cook until the broccoli is tender. Season with salt to taste.

While cooking the vegetables, prepare the couscous according to package directions. When the vegetables are done, spoon them over the couscous. We serve this dish with a simple Middle Eastern salad and pita bread.

Authors' note: We fix this recipe different ways — vary the vegetables and use fresh or canned tomatoes, for example. But we don't vary the proportions of the spices; we always enjoy this blend.

Marinara Sauce

SERVES FOUR TO FIVE

Marinara sauce simply refers to a sauce made from the vegetables that sailors brought back to Italy from the New World. So any tomato sauce may be called marinara sauce, but ours has that fresh, softly cooked taste like those served in Utica and Rome, New York. We use less oil than most recipes call for, cooking the sauce in a large, nonstick skillet and letting the juicy chopped onion provide its own liquid.

  1 large onion
  3 large garlic cloves
  2 tablespoons olive oil
 10 large Roma tomatoes, peeled and seeded

½ cup fresh basil, sliced into narrow strips
½ teaspoon dried oregano
2 tablespoons parsley, chopped
1 pound pasta, cooked

Chop the onion and garlic in a food processor and cook them in the olive oil until just limp. (We save the onion- and garlic-flavored juice and add it to soups.) Chop the tomatoes coarsely in the same processor and drain them in a sieve. Add the drained tomatoes to the onion-garlic mixture and sauté another five or ten minutes. Halfway through, add the basil, oregano, and parsley. Serve over a pound of pasta (we prefer linguine).

You'll note that we don't list salt as an ingredient. That's because we've found that the one mistake you can make with this recipe is to oversalt it. It's better to add salt to taste at the table.

This sauce freezes quite well, so we make three or four batches at one time and freeze them in plastic containers.

Corn "Hollandaise"

Our young friend Becky Slattery, who studied at the Natural Gourmet Cooking School in New York City, sent us this unusual recipe. We tried it on broccoli. It was beautiful, with the color and consistency of hollandaise sauce, in addition to being healthy and quite delicious.

4 ears corn
    lemon juice to taste
    salt and pepper to taste

Remove the kernels from the cobs. Puree the kernels in a processor, processing in small batches. Squeeze the "milk" produced through a dish towel or a piece of cheesecloth. Cook this "milk" in a saucepan for 10 to 15 minutes, stirring constantly, until it has the consistency of a sauce. Then transfer the sauce to a double boiler, just to keep it warm, and season to taste with the lemon juice, salt, and pepper. At this point, you may also add a little butter or margarine. Serve warm over vegetables, meat, poultry, or fish.

Garden Vegetable Casserole

SERVES EIGHT

Cecile Turner Wood shares this delicious recipe, which was printed in the Grand Rapids Press. *Cecile is a home economist with the Kent County Extension Service of Michigan State University. Her popular column in the press features tips and recipes for low-cost, healthy eating.*

    6 cups unpeeled red potatoes, cubed (about two pounds)
    1 cup carrots, diagonally sliced
    1 cup fresh green beans, sliced
    ½ cup onion, chopped
  2½ cups skim milk, divided
    2 teaspoons chicken bouillon granules
    ¼ cup flour
  1½ cups (6 ounces) reduced-fat, sharp cheddar cheese, shredded and divided
    1 teaspoon dried dill weed or 1 tablespoon fresh dill
    1 teaspoon dried whole marjoram
      or 1 tablespoon fresh marjoram
    1 teaspoon dried basil or 1 tablespoon fresh basil
    ¼ teaspoon pepper
    ¼ teaspoon dry mustard
    1 cup sliced zucchini
      vegetable cooking spray
    1 large, unpeeled tomato, thinly sliced

Boil the potatoes for eight minutes or until tender yet firm; drain and set aside. Arrange the carrots and green beans on a plate, then cover with vented plastic wrap and microwave on high for five minutes. (Alternatively, the vegetables may be steamed in a saucepan.) Set aside. In a nonstick saucepan, cook the onions for about 3 minutes. Add 1½ cups of the skim milk and the chicken bouillon. Shake the flour and the remaining cup of the skim milk together and stir into the onion mixture. Cook over medium heat, stirring constantly until thickened. Remove from heat and stir in ¾ cup of the cheese and the dill, marjoram, basil, pepper, and dry mustard.

Combine the potatoes, carrots, green beans, and zucchini in a 13 × 9 × 2-inch glass baking dish coated with cooking spray. Pour the cheese sauce over the vegetables and bake, uncovered, at 350° for twenty minutes. Arrange the tomato slices on top of the casserole, sprinkle with the remaining ¾ cup of cheese, and bake an additional five minutes.

Ratatouille Pizza

"MAKES SIX PERSONAL PIZZAS (AND GREAT MEMORIES)"

Karin Orr is one of the best-known personalities in West Michigan. She is a longtime lifestyle columnist for the Grand Rapids Press *and has a weekly food column in the paper as well. She also is a TV chef on WGVU, Grand Rapids' PBS channel. "Sorry this is so-o-o long a recipe," she told us, "but it is delicious." She went on to say that "the best thing about this recipe is that it uses everything from the garden. The crust is also good separately, as focaccia, and the filling is a fabulous ratatouille. But together, they're unbeatable."*

CRUST (focaccia):
- 2 packages active dry yeast
- 4 tablespoons lukewarm water
- ¼ cup sugar
- ¼ cup garlic, minced
- 2 tablespoons fresh parsley, coarsely chopped
- 1 tablespoon fresh basil, coarsely chopped
- ¼ cup best-quality olive oil
- 8 cups high-gluten flour
- 1½ tablespoons salt
- 2½ cups water

FILLING (ratatouille):
- 2 tablespoons best-quality olive oil
- 1 large sweet onion, diced
- 2 cloves garlic, crushed
- 1 red sweet pepper, coarsely chopped
- 1 green sweet pepper, coarsely chopped

1 small eggplant, diced

1 small zucchini, diced

1 small summer squash, diced

4 (or more) ripe tomatoes, peeled, seeded, and chopped

1 tablespoon fresh basil, chopped, or 1 teaspoon dried basil

1 bay leaf

1 teaspoon fresh thyme leaves, snipped,
   or ½ teaspoon dried thyme

1 teaspoon fresh oregano, minced,
   or ½ teaspoon dried oregano

1 teaspoon chicken bouillon granules

1 teaspoon red wine vinegar

   salt and pepper to taste

   freshly grated Parmesan cheese or crumbled feta or
      Gorgonzola to taste

   fresh basil, chopped, to garnish

To make the pizza crust, proof the yeast by mixing it with the four tablespoons of water. Add the sugar and stir to dissolve. When the mixture bubbles (in 5 to 10 minutes), add the garlic, parsley, basil, and olive oil. Stir the flour and salt together, then pour the yeast mixture into the flour mixture. Add the 2½ cups of water and mix thoroughly. Turn the dough out onto a floured surface and knead until slightly tacky (10 to 12 minutes). Place in an oiled bowl, cover, and let rise about one hour. Then punch down and refrigerate another hour (or until ready to make pizzas).

For the ratatouille filling, heat the olive oil in a large pan, such as a Dutch oven. Sauté the onion and garlic until tender but not browned. Add the red and green peppers, eggplant, zucchini, and squash. Cook, covered, for about 10 minutes, stirring occasionally. Then add the tomatoes, basil, bay leaf, thyme, oregano, chicken bouillon granules, vinegar, and salt and pepper, and simmer, covered, for another 10 to 12 minutes. Uncover and carefully cook off the excess moisture. Remove the bay leaf.

To make the pizzas: Divide the dough into six pieces and roll each out on a floured surface to ¼-inch thick and 6 inches in diameter. Place on a pan or cookie sheet dusted with cornmeal and bake at 325° for 10 to 15 minutes, then remove them. Using a slotted spoon, place the desired amount of ratatouille filling on each pizza and sprinkle with cheese. Then bake 5 to 10 minutes, or until the cheese bubbles. Remove from the oven, sprinkle with the fresh basil, and serve.

Karin Orr's note: If you're pressed for time, you can substitute commercially prepared focaccia crusts.

Entrée de Legumes à la Kerrytown Bistro

SERVES ONE

One of our favorite Ann Arbor restaurants is the Kerrytown Bistro, located in a building adjacent to the Kerrytown Market. It seems to us that this restaurant always uses fresh vegetables and that everything is individually cooked to order just for us. When I (Nelle) asked for the recipe for the superb vegetable dish I had just eaten, the owners of the Bistro, Otto and Mary Shea Gago, came to our table to talk to us and find out what we were doing. To my surprise, it was the same Mary Shea who had attended East Grand Rapids High with our daughter. Otto and Mary were most gracious, and willing to share this recipe with you.

It sounds complicated for everyday use, but each vegetable in the mix is delicious and could serve as the basis of a dish by itself. And the recipe confirms our belief that the Bistro truly cooks to order. We present it the way Otto and Mary gave it to us.

After brushing with olive oil, lightly salt and pepper 1 medium slice of eggplant, 2 elongated ovals of zucchini, and 2 of summer squash, then grill with a pattern and arrange nicely on a plate. Keep these warm. Next, stuff a tomato with roasted, marinated strips of bell peppers, top with crumbled chèvre cheese, and broil. Place the tomato in the center of a plate, and just below this, arrange braised red-and-white cabbage. (To make braised cabbage, lightly sauté thin slices of onion in olive oil with fresh coriander seed, salt, and white pepper. Then add sliced cabbage and sauté lightly. Add a splash of chardonnay, a large splash of white-wine vinegar, and enough granulated sugar to adjust the acidity. Cover and place in a 350° oven until tender, making sure there is enough liquid to keep the cabbage from sticking. Transfer the cabbage to the plate.) Finish the plate with blanched spinach, quartered red potatoes preboiled and then pan roasted, and a blend of wild and white rice.

Authors' note: The chef of the Bistro recommends that if you serve wine with this dish, you choose a well-balanced chardonnay such as Edna Valley or Simi.

Zucchini Fromage

SERVES EIGHT

It's always the nicest people who respond best to requests, and Ann Wells, the food editor of the Grand Rapids Press, *is among the nicest. We sent her a form letter, devised by our publisher, asking for a recipe. She responded with three recipes, plus a handwritten note of encouragement that ended with "Thanks for asking me," as though we were doing her the favor. It's the reverse. When you try this fromage, you'll know that Ann is not only a nice person, she's a fine cook. (And her work makes buying the paper a bargain.)*

     5-6 cups zucchini, cut in ¼-inch slices
  1-1½ cups mushrooms, sliced
     1 bunch green onions, sliced, both white and green parts
     4 eggs
     ½ cup sour cream
     ¼ cup Parmesan cheese, grated
         salt and pepper to taste
         dill weed to taste
         additional Parmesan cheese, if desired

Grease a 9 × 13-inch glass pan. Layer in the zucchini, mushrooms, and green onions. Beat together the eggs, sour cream, cheese, salt, pepper, and dill. Pour this sauce over the vegetables, sprinkle with additional cheese if desired, and bake 30 to 40 minutes at 350°, or until the vegetables are tender and the casserole is browned on top and bubbling.

Don's note: If you make this frequently, you might avoid the feeling that the world has too much zucchini, but like other good things in life, this recipe is not fat free or cholesterol free.

Simple Zucchini

SERVES EIGHT

Ann Wells, the food editor of the Grand Rapids Press, *offers this use for zucchini, along with her sinful Zucchini Fromage recipe. If you're watching your fat intake, you might like this spicy dish better, but you ought to try them both.*

 5-6 cups zucchini, sliced
  1 large onion, sliced
 2-3 tomatoes, sliced
  1 teaspoon red pepper flakes (or amount to taste)
 1-2 cups mozzarella cheese, grated
 1½ teaspoons dried basil, crumbled

Layer half of the zucchini, onion slices, and tomatoes in a 9 × 13-inch glass casserole (greased). Sprinkle with half the red pepper flakes, half the grated cheese, and half the basil. Repeat with a second layer or more, if needed. Bake in a 350° oven for 45 to 60 minutes, and run the dish under the broiler to brown the cheese, if desired.

Gruyère Tomato Soufflés

SERVES TEN

Ann Wells, the food editor of the Grand Rapids Press, *says of this recipe, "These Gruyère-stuffed tomatoes are a favorite, wonderful with fresh tomatoes from the garden (and a great way to add zip to winter tomatoes and color to a dinner plate)."*

 10 large tomatoes
   salt to taste
 3-4 eggs

12 ounces grated Gruyère cheese
   pepper to taste

Cut off about ¼- to ½-inch from the tops of the tomatoes and remove the seeds, then salt the insides. In a small bowl, beat the eggs. Add the Gruyère and pepper and mix well. Fill the tomatoes with the egg/cheese mixture and bake in a 300° to 325° oven for 30 minutes, or until the soufflés are firm and golden.

Ann's note: This is one of those recipes that can be easily cut in size or increased. And the tomatoes can be filled several hours before baking.

Peach Cobbler

SERVES FOUR TO SIX

Iris Mann of Mann Farms in Fennville has adapted this recipe from her Betty Crocker cookbook. Her husband, John, loves it, and chose it to share with us.

FILLING:
½ cup sugar
1 tablespoon cornstarch
¼ teaspoon ground cinnamon
4 cups peaches, peeled and sliced
   (about six medium freestones)
1 teaspoon lemon juice

TOPPING:
3 tablespoons vegetable shortening
1 cup all-purpose flour (if using self-rising flour,
   omit the baking powder and salt that follow)
1 tablespoon sugar
1½ teaspoons baking powder
½ teaspoon salt
½ cup milk

Preheat the oven to 400°. Mix the ½ cup sugar, cornstarch, and cinnamon in a two-quart saucepan, then stir in the peaches and lemon juice. Cook, stirring constantly, until the mixture thickens. Bring to a boil and continue stirring for one minute. Pour the mixture into an ungreased two-quart glass casserole and put it in the oven.

To make the topping, cut the shortening into the flour, add the tablespoon of sugar, the baking powder, and the salt, and continue cutting until the mixture resembles fine crumbs. Stir in the milk. Then drop by spoonfuls onto the hot peach mixture and bake until the topping is golden brown, about 30 minutes.

Peach Clafouti

SERVES FOUR

Clare Hempel, Food Service Director for the Reformed Bible College, says that this is a marvelous dessert on its own, but also very good when served with whipped cream, vanilla ice cream, or vanilla yogurt.

1¼ cups milk
3 eggs
1 tablespoon vanilla
2 tablespoons rum (optional)
¼ teaspoon salt
⅔ cup all-purpose flour, sifted
3 cups peaches, peeled and sliced
⅓ cup granulated sugar
½ teaspoon cinnamon
powdered sugar

Place all ingredients, except the peaches, sugar, and cinnamon, in a blender jar in the order given. Blend at top speed for one minute. Lightly butter an 11 × 7-inch glass baking dish and pour a ¼-inch layer of batter in the dish. Set over moderate heat until a film of batter has set in the dish, then remove from heat. Spread the sliced peaches over the batter and sprinkle with the granulated sugar mixed with the cinnamon. Then pour on the rest of the batter and smooth the surface with the back of a spoon.

Place the dish in the middle of a 350° oven and bake for about 45 minutes. The clafouti is done when the top is puffed and brown, and a knife comes out clean when plunged into its center. The clafouti will sink slightly as it cools. Serve it at room temperature or when it is still slightly warm, sprinkled with powdered sugar.

Ike's Blackberry Brioche Pudding

SERVES EIGHT

Chef Jimmy Schmidt is the proprietor of Detroit's renowned Rattlesnake Club, Très Vite, Cocina del Sol, and Buster's Bay. His book, Cooking for All Seasons, *was published by Macmillan and is available in most good bookstores. This busy chef still has time to write a regular column called "Jimmy Schmidt's Cooking Class," often featuring recipes that use fresh produce, for the* Detroit Free Press. *This blackberry recipe first appeared in one of his columns in August 1992. Thinking back to a childhood experience, he wrote, "Blackberries always were harder to locate in the thick underbrush than their more brightly colored cousins, but for me it was worth risking poison ivy to enjoy their deep, rich flavor." If it's worth that risk, it's certainly worth sharing his recipe with you.*

He suggests a number of other uses for blackberries, including plain for breakfast or with a dollop of whipped cream for dessert, but he says he prefers the flavor of cooked raspberries.

    8 cups fresh brioche, cubed (or other sweet egg-bread)
    2 pints fresh blackberries (or related dark berries)
    6 whole eggs, beaten
    3 egg yolks, beaten
    1 cup granulated sugar
    2 tablespoons vanilla extract
 1½ cups milk, scalded
 1½ cups light cream (or half-and-half), scalded
       confectioners' sugar
    8 scoops French vanilla ice cream
    8 large sprigs fresh mint for garnish

Preheat the oven to 350°. In a buttered 9 × 13-inch glass baking dish, place half the cubed brioche evenly across the bottom. Cover with half the blackberries and repeat the layers with the remaining fruit and brioche cubes.

In a medium bowl, combine the eggs, yolks, sugar, and vanilla. Gradually stir in the hot scalded milk and cream, then pour the mixture over the blackberries and brioche. With a spoon or spatula, press down until most of the mixture has been absorbed by the brioche. Bake on the lower oven rack until firm and golden, about 25 to 30 minutes. Test by inserting a skewer or pick into the center. The center should be hot, and the skewer should come out clean. Cool slightly on a cake rack.

To serve, cut the warm pudding into squares. Transfer to plates with a spoon and dust with confectioners' sugar sifted through a fine mesh strainer. Put a scoop of ice cream beside each square of pudding, and garnish with the mint.

Peach Chutney

MAKES FIVE PINTS

For years, Clare Hempel, Food Service Director for the Reformed Bible College, has given us jars of his peach chutney as gifts for almost any occasion. Never before, however, has he shared his recipe. We offer it here as a gift to you. Serve it with curries or as a garnish for just about anything else.

     2 quarts peaches, peeled and sliced
     2 Granny Smith apples, peeled and chopped
     2 cups yellow onions, finely chopped
     2 cups seedless green or red grapes
     1 cup golden raisins
 1½ cups brown sugar, firmly packed
     1 cup cider vinegar
     2 garlic cloves, peeled and pressed
     1 teaspoon ground coriander
     1 teaspoon salt
     1 teaspoon nutmeg

½ teaspoon ground cloves

¼ teaspoon cayenne pepper

4 ounces crystallized ginger, finely chopped

½ cup molasses

Combine all ingredients in a large non-aluminum pan. Simmer for two hours, stirring often to prevent burning or scorching. When the mixture is cooked, pour it into hot, sterilized jars, leaving a quarter-inch of head space in each jar before sealing. Then process the jars in a water bath for twenty minutes. Store them in a cool place. Keep in mind that the chutney is best when it's allowed to mellow for six months.

Fruit and Honey Chutney

MAKES FIVE PINTS

Pat Bourdo of the Woodland Herb Farm near Northport blends and sells the finest herb vinegars you'll ever find. In addition, she sells dried and fresh herbs, spice mixes, exotic chutneys, and a changing list of other products as new ideas surface in Pat's creative mind. She also suggests how to use herbs, and that's always free and pleasant advice. She thought of this recipe, published in her Woodland Herb Farm Condiment Cookbook, as soon as we told her we were watching our fat and salt intake. It features zucchini, which Pat assures us is lowest in sodium of all garden vegetables.

6 cups zucchini, coarsely ground (do not peel, but if the zucchini are large, you may want to seed them)

1 cup tart apples, cored but not peeled, coarsely ground

1 cup pears, peeled and cored, coarsely ground

1 onion, finely ground

¾ pound seedless raisins or dates, ground

1 tablespoon celery seed

1 cup honey

1 lemon, juice and grated rind

1⅓ cups cider vinegar

⅓ cup (undiluted) frozen orange juice concentrate, thawed

Combine all ingredients in a large non-aluminum pot and simmer until thickened, stirring occasionally. When the mixture is cooked, pour it into hot, sterilized jars, leaving a quarter-inch of head space in each jar before sealing. Then process the jars in a bath of boiling water for 10 minutes. The flavor of this chutney improves after a week or two.

Lemon-Cucumber Marmalade

MAKES THREE PINTS

Pat Bourdo and her husband, Jon, operate the Woodland Herb Farm and Culinary Herb Shop. Curiously, one of the recipes Pat most wanted to share was this marmalade, which has no herbs. Note, please, that this recipe was first published in Pat's book, The Woodland Herb Farm Condiment Cookbook, *which is available at bookstores and at their showroom.*

- 2 cups cucumbers (about 1½ pounds), peeled and finely chopped
- 4 cups sugar
- ⅓ cup fresh lemon juice
- 2 tablespoons grated lemon rind
- green food coloring (optional)
- 1 package liquid fruit pectin (3 ounces)

In a large saucepan, combine the chopped cucumbers, sugar, lemon juice, and rind. Mix well and place over high heat. Add the food coloring, if desired, bring to a full, rolling boil, and boil hard for one minute, stirring constantly. Remove from the heat and immediately stir in the fruit pectin. Skim off the foam that forms and stir for five minutes to cool the mixture slightly and to prevent floating fruit and vegetables. Then pour the mixture into hot, sterilized jars, leaving a quarter-inch of head space in each jar before sealing. Process the jars in a bath of boiling water for 5 minutes.

Freezer Corn

There are many ways to freeze corn, including corn on the cob, but most of the farmers we talked to suggest freezing kernels. A number volunteered recipes, and surprisingly enough, they were all slightly different. We've included a recipe from Betty Nitz of the Grand Rapids Fulton Street Farmers' Market, and one from Patty Miller of the Old Barn Market at Miller Orchard Farm near Coloma. Both recipes produce fine frozen corn, so try them both to see which taste you prefer.

BETTY NITZ'S RECIPE:

16 cups raw sweet-corn kernels
2½ teaspoons salt
1 tablespoon sugar
1 stick butter
2-3 cups water

Combine all ingredients and simmer for five minutes. Let the corn cool in the pan, then bag in plastic freezer bags and freeze.

PATTY MILLER'S RECIPE:

1 stick butter
2 tablespoons sugar
1 teaspoon salt
2 tablespoons water
8 cups sweet-corn kernels

Melt the butter and add the rest of the ingredients except the corn. Cut the corn off the cob fresh — do not cook first. Put the corn in a pan, make a well in the center, and add the butter mixture. Cook until soupy, cool, and freeze.

Home-Frozen Michigan Peaches

MAKES SIX PINTS

Deanna House, home economist and author of More House Specialties, *shares this recipe from that cookbook. "This plan for freezing
peaches," she says, "is a 'gift' to students in my Portage Community
Education Basic Microwave classes. . . . It uses a very light syrup,
which produces a quality product with wonderful peach flavor."*

> 1 quart water
> 1 cup sugar
> 3 teaspoons vitamin C fruit protector
> 15-20 fresh, ripe peaches
> 6 full-pint plastic freezer containers

In a medium saucepan, bring the water and sugar to a boil, stirring
occasionally, and then chill the syrup produced. Peel the peaches
by dipping 3 or 4 at a time in boiling water for 15 to 20 seconds
until the skins loosen, then chilling them quickly in ice water or
very cold water and peeling. Next add vitamin C fruit protector
to the cold syrup and stir well.

Fill the freezer containers one-third full with this cold syrup.
Slice the peaches directly into the freezer containers, completely
covering the fruit with the cold syrup, but leaving a half-inch of
head space in each container. Keep the peaches submerged in the
syrup by placing a generous piece of crumpled freezer paper or
waxed paper under the lid of each container. Cover, label, date,
and freeze immediately. (If you're using a microwave, you can
make the syrup by microwaving it on full power for five to eight
minutes, stirring once.)

FALL

FOR US, THERE'S SOMETHING A LITTLE SAD ABOUT AU-
tumn, a season that signals the end of summer and heralds the onset
of winter. At the same time, fall is an exhilarating season, with its
colors of deep, bright reds, oranges, and yellows. And in Michigan
these colors parade through the forests and up the hills, bringing
legions of tourists to view the autumn leaves. So from mid-September
through October is the time for you to get your camera and join the
busloads of people on color tours.

But the reds of maples and oaks fade next to the brilliant
reds of apples and tomatoes, and the yellows of birch and beech
pale when compared with the yellows and oranges of squashes
and pumpkins. So fall is also the time to load up the kids and take
them to the farms and farm markets of Michigan. Try going to
different regions. See the bean and beet harvests in the thumb of
the state, or the apple harvest along Fruit Ridge. Go to Grant. The
whole town smells like onions, and they sell more hundred-pound
sacks than three-pound bags.

*Fall Harvest
Activities*

You'll find that the farmers smile a great deal during this
season. They know what their work has produced, and while they
might begin to worry about getting everything in before an early
frost, their crops are ready to harvest and sell.

When you see all that they're selling, you'll smile back at the
farmers. And your kids will smile when they find that some of the
farmers have set up old-fashioned entertainments to help celebrate
the fall harvest. Kids will love the hayrides, the petting zoos, and
picking their own pumpkins from the fields.

During the week, farmers welcome school groups who sup-
posedly are there to learn about healthy vegetables, but who are
most attracted by the same things your kids love. And after school,
a favorite activity for Girl Scout Troops is a trip to farms and cider

mills. Robinette's has so many of these groups coming through during the cider season that the owners decorate the snack bar by posting the thank-you letters from the kids.

Many farms provide some kind of food — mostly doughnuts, caramel apples, and cider. Others have set aside picnic areas with tables.

The Christmas Cove Farm near Northport grows some most interesting "antique" apple varieties, some rarely seen today, including one beloved by Thomas Jefferson. The owners package them for sale in their Apple Barn Gift Shop.

The Sprik farm, north of Grand Rapids, offers a chance to see huge draft horses and bison. And it's exciting to see close up these animals that were so important in our history.

The Franklin Cider Mill began operations five years before Michigan was admitted to the Union and is now a national historic site. More than 15,000 people visit on fall weekends to tour the mill, savor the cider, and feast on apple pie and candied apples.

Orchard Hill in Lowell remembers rural history and offers

A hot cup of cider on a cool day is one of fall's pleasures.

entertaining wagon rides, deer feeding, and lessons on scarecrow making.

Honeyflow Farm in Lapeer County lets you pick twenty different varieties of grapes, plus dip your own honey from the farm's tank.

Cripps Fruit Farm in Alpena offers hayrides to the pumpkin patch and has an animal petting farm.

Klackle Orchards in Greenville has hayrides and a scheduled pig roast. They even hold a meet featuring radio-controlled model airplanes.

Aspin Farms near Swartz Creek offers horse-drawn wagon rides and presents country music shows on Friday nights.

Wiard's Orchards near Ypsilanti offers a "country fair" on weekends, which includes face painting for kids, pony rides, and fire-engine rides. There's also a craft fair, live music, and more.

Heartwarming Acres, in Ingham County near Mason, is a sheep farm that offers a full line of produce at an honor stand. But what is most unique is that it offers classes in quilting, knitting, crocheting, and other crafts. That's great adult entertainment.

This is an incomplete list of fall activities on the farm, but it's long enough to make the point that wherever you happen to live in Michigan, you can go to a farm for fruit, fun, and family activities. Check the papers to see what's available in your area, and be prepared to spend the day. Perhaps you might pack a picnic to enjoy on a quiet farm, and have your own harvest celebration.

Remember that it's usually crowded at farm stands in the fall, and that farmers expand their parking areas to their lawns, meadows, and road shoulders, even encroaching on their normal parking areas to display the extravagant abundance of their fall harvest. Where once you would have parked, there's a pile of pumpkins or a bin of apples. Some farm stands — Under the Pines in Walker, for example — abandon tables when making their displays, showing onions, cabbages, squash, pumpkins, and fruit in bushels, crates, and bins.

At this time of year, flower growers have harvested all their statice, baby's breath, bittersweet, and strawflowers, and show big, beautiful bunches of the dried flowers. You can combine these with gourds, miniature pumpkins, dried grains, three-inch ears of

Dried Flowers

*A mother-and-daughter team proudly display
their colorful selection of dried flowers.*

popcorn, and Indian corn to make centerpieces. You'll find a myriad of colors to fit your decorating scheme.

We wondered where this pretty harvest comes from, and so we took a walk with Martin Andre around the farm that he and his family run for their business, Flowers of the Field on the East Beltline. The size of just one of the farms devoted to filling decorating needs amazed us. We had thought that decorative farm plants would probably just be a sideline for the farmer.

Martin took us through his cornfields, and we saw corn that grew two feet tall, corn that grew twelve feet tall, corn with purple stalks. Martin explained the varieties: "We grow this for the tassels, and we grow this for shucking. We have to cut all this by hand too. The shucking machines tie the stalks too near the top for modern decorating." Martin also told us that they grow Indian corn in numerous varieties to satisfy customer demand for colors, and he noted that "deer really love pumpkins and gourds, and can ruin a crop." We learned, in short, that farming to provide flowers and decorative items requires a serious effort.

Flower growers also present for the first time in the fall their harvest of flowering hardy mums, potted for you to plant outside. Blossoms in shades of white, purple, yellow, and deep orange are common. The Flower Farm in St. Clair has a mind-boggling display of these mums, with what must be thousands of plants for sale.

On the weekends at municipal markets, farmers who normally drove one truck to market now take two, surrounding their vehicles and display stalls with their produce. The nursery and flower growers do the same, surrounding their stalls with hardy mums in full bloom.

Market shoppers (you'll meet lots of people you know) block aisles to stoop and inspect the bushels of tomatoes and potatoes under the tables. They squeeze the plums and the pears. They make many trips to the car, because fall is the last chance to make preserves from the fruit and can the vegetables. And they buy apples.

In Michigan, fall is the time for the apple harvest, a time of spectacular abundance. Hundreds of apple varieties are picked and sold at hundreds of farm stands around Michigan. In fact, Herb and Liz Teichman of Tree-Mendus Fruit in Eau Claire say they grow over two hundred kinds of apples — some are ancestral stocks, and others, recently developed hybrids.

That's not surprising, since some reference books list 3,000 varieties of apples grown in North America. These apples range in color from green to brilliant red, in shape from round to what can only be described as a red Delicious shape, in taste from tart to sweet, with some a little spicy, and in texture from juicy to dry.

As a result, "What is the best apple?" has no real answer. Some apples are better for cooking, others better for eating. But which you might like for a specific purpose is, by and large, a matter of personal taste.

Generally, if you like a sweet apple to eat, it's tough to beat a red Delicious, but Shirley Hartstock, of Klackle Orchards in Greenville, suggests you might find that their very popular Gala apple, a new hybrid of the golden Delicious and the pippin, is sweeter. Or try a Jonagold apple, a hybrid of the Jonathan and the golden Delicious. Our favorite eating apple is a bright red Empire apple, which is sweet, juicy, and crisp. But it's tough to pass by a perfect polished McIntosh. For both eating and cooking, our East Coast daughter loves Macouns, which have a particular sweet-tart taste, but they're rare in Michigan.

For cooking, Jonathans are great, as are the early Granny Smiths, Cortlands, Paula Reds, Ida Reds, and Northern Spys.

And you know the old saw about keeping the doctor away, so eat an apple every day, at least through the fall. This healthy benefit of apple eating can be extended by replacing the oil in your muffin or cake recipe with the same volume of applesauce, thus reducing fat in the recipe. We first heard of that in an advertisement for Mott's applesauce, and it works. We've also used applesauce instead of oil in our Thanksgiving turkey stuffing, and that worked too. We've included a recipe for homemade applesauce, in case you want to try this new approach. If not, applesauce is worth making just to eat, and it freezes well.

Now is the time to enjoy making and eating the old-favorite apple desserts — pies, crisps, tarts — and to remember that a microwave makes baked apples a fast-food treat. And this is the best time to enjoy using apples in cooking to flavor main dishes. We've included a recipe for preparing cider-glazed chicken with apple slices.

Pears Apples and pears mix well. Bartlett pears are early, and are yellow-green, rosy skinned, or even red. They're large, juicy pears, suitable for both cooking and eating. Compared with other varieties, they're soft and sweet. Bosc pears, our favorite, are a russet color, and they're a little smaller, a little tarter, and firmer than the Bartletts. Most farmers think these, like the Bartletts, are fine for both eating and cooking. Anjou pears are good, firm pears common in Michigan. Other varieties, all with their special qualities, include Clapp, Comice, and the tiny Seckels. Kieffer pears are called "hard winter pears," and ripen slowly, so if you store them in a cool place, they'll last most of the winter.

Ripe pears don't store well, although they may be kept in the refrigerator for a couple of days. And farmers pick and display pears before they're ripe; in fact, one farmer we know goes so far as to advise us never to buy a ripe pear. So look for firm fruit, with no soft spots, to ripen on the kitchen counter at home. When a pear smells like a pear, it's ready.

Cooking with pears is much the same as cooking with apples, and a number of farmers told us that the best applesauce is made by mixing pears in with the apples.

A variety of grapes are grown in Michigan, from table grapes to vinifera and French hybrid grapes used in the production of wine. Still popular are native American grapes like Concord and Niagara, but newer seedless varieties are being introduced into the Michigan produce mix. Niagara grapes are used primarily for white grape juice, and Concord grapes are still the favorite for grape jelly, an essential in our "world famous" peanut-butter-and-jelly sandwiches. You can pick your own Concords at a number of farms; in fact, at Seitsema Orchards on Three Mile Road, that's the only u-pick crop.

Grapes

Today, the most excitement surrounding the grape harvest

*An abundance of apples and pears fills the
makeshift tables of this farm market.*

comes from the Michigan wines, some of which have gotten so good that they regularly win medals in national and international competitions. In fact, the appellations "Lake Michigan Shore," "Leelanau Peninsula," and "Old Mission Peninsula" are now federally recognized and registered marks of quality. The names indicate the lake-tempered climate and good soil of these areas, perfect for growing wine grapes.

Note that wine takes time to mature, so the wine traditionally released in the fall may be from grapes harvested two or three years before.

Usually, wine makers don't produce more grapes than they need; if they do, they typically will contract with other wineries to sell their excess crop. A few will sell grapes or juice to amateur wine makers; Lemon Creek Vineyards in Berrien Springs even makes its "wine grapes" available to u-pickers. It offers a unique opportunity to pick French hybrid wine grapes, Riesling grapes, and even the ubiquitous Concord grapes.

Michigan Wines   Michigan wine makers are proudest of their whites: Rieslings, Seyval Blancs, Videl Blancs, Vignoles, and Chardonnays. Proprietary wines — for example, Leland's Good Harbor Fish Town White and Omena's Leelanau Wine Cellars Vis-à-Vis White — are blends of these basic varieties.

The growing season in Michigan is a little short for red-wine grapes, but wine makers have produced creditable Beaujolais-style wines using a mix of Foch grapes and Baco Noir grapes. Some wineries making this kind of wine have taken advantage of the fad for "nouveau" wine, releasing it in November to coincide with the French wine release.

The Chancellor grape produces a claret-style wine, and Doug Welsch, wine maker at Fenn Valley in Fennville, reports that his Chancellor wine has won gold and silver medals in "literally every wine competition we entered." Like claret, this wine improves with aging.

The Chambourcin grapes make a fine Burgundy-style wine. This grape ripens late, so look for this wine from south Michigan wineries — and you may not find it every year. The most consistent supplier is the St. Julian Wine Company in Paw Paw, which has it almost every year.

Michigan wineries also produce a variety of fruit wines, with

Tabor Hill is a wonderful place to eat as well as sample wine.

cherry predominating. In addition, wine vinegars, grape juices, and nonalcoholic wines are all available from Michigan wineries. Diana Welsch of Fenn Valley, one of the leaders in the development of dealcoholized wine, says, "You get full wine taste, with about a half percent alcohol. The only thing lacking is the 'bite' alcohol adds to the taste."

The wineries of Michigan and their tasting rooms are pleasant places to visit in the fall. All serve crackers at the tasting bar, and most have some food available to eat with what you drink. Fenn Valley has cheeses to munch with your wine, and a pleasant deck next to the vineyard, so you can sit outside and enjoy the day. Chateau Chantal on the Old Mission Peninsula offers wine, fruit, cheeses, and "sunsets on the terrace." Tabor Hill in Buchanan has a full-service restaurant overlooking their vineyard. (Our favorite dish was the Sautéed Chicken Raspberry, but the recipe is a secret.) Tabor Hill celebrates fall with a jazz fest and a grape stomp in the vineyard, at which they serve casual food.

The owners of Heart of the Vineyard Winery in Baroda have

turned their old farmhouse into a bed and breakfast, offering rooms with "romantic views of the vineyard." They have an outdoor hot tub made from an old wine vat once owned by Al Capone.

The Warners of Warner Vineyards in Paw Paw operate an indoor/outdoor bistro restaurant, which Lynne Warner says "has a real European feel." We were sniffling when we last visited, so we ate inside, where Lynne prescribed the chicken soup as "a sure cure for a fall cold." Most often we eat something like their apple-chicken sausage outside on their extensive, multileveled deck alongside the Paw Paw River.

The Warners decorate the deck with wine casks planted with herbs (Lynne says it takes ninety flats to fill them), which they can use in cooking. In the fall, growers also bring raspberries to Lynne's door.

At this time, raspberries make a return to market, and most fruits of summer are still available. Locally grown native plums make their first appearance, and you can get both damson and Italian prune plums in the fall.

Late Summer Vegetables
Summer vegetables also are still available, only they're bigger and more abundant. Cauliflower heads range up to fifteen inches in diameter, green cabbages get so large that they're hard to lift, carrots can grow to be a foot long and an inch in diameter, and zucchini looks like it can be sold for use as bats in Little League baseball. Brussels sprouts make their first appearance and are sold by the pound or by the stalk, an increasingly popular way to buy them. Broccoli is massed in huge piles on the farmers' tables, and tomatoes are sold in bushel baskets. Beans, too, are sold by the bushel, but no longer are they labeled "first picking."

Russet potatoes, the baking kind, reach the markets in early fall, as do yams and sweet potatoes. Giant turnips, rutabagas, and parsnips also attract attention as shoppers begin to think in terms of soups, stews, and roasts surrounded by vegetables. Chips made from root vegetables have become trendy to serve. Just slice thinly whatever vegetable(s) you choose, toss with some cooking oil, and roast in a moderate oven.

Squash
The most visible vegetables of fall are squash and pumpkins. The hard-skinned squash comes in several varieties — butternut (winter) squash, buttercup squash, the picturesque acorn squash, and turban squash. These are all smooth-surfaced squash. The

bumpy-skinned green or orange squash is Hubbard squash, which can grow so large that farmers will often sell it to you by the chunk. You can also buy an oval yellow squash called spaghetti squash. After cooking it, you can shred its flesh longitudinally until it looks like pasta. In fact, you can serve it like pasta, covered with meat or tomato sauce.

Squash can be baked or boiled. If you bake it, you can serve the halves in a variety of ways — topped with maple syrup, stuffed with a meat-and-rice mixture, filled with peas. If you boil squash, scoop out the flesh, mash it, and serve it piping hot with melted butter. Some people like the plain taste of squash; others drown it in sweet sauces. Yams may also be baked or boiled and the meat mashed. You can boil slices of yams, dot them with butter and marshmallows, and create "a favorite for Thanksgiving."

Pumpkins come two ways: for cooking and for decorating. The cooking pumpkins are small and often greenish. The New England pie pumpkin is a commonly grown variety in Michigan. It has a particularly sweet flesh and makes excellent pies.

Pumpkins

The decorating pumpkins are what attract the kids. Any weekday during the fall, you'll see teachers at farm markets, taking their nursery-school classes on field trips. Each child clutches enough change to buy a small pumpkin, and perhaps a candy apple.

It takes a large farming industry to supply all these pumpkins, and the growers must plant a range of varieties to satisfy customers' individual tastes concerning size, shape, and color. Martin Andre of Flowers of the Field has planted a field of Long Boy pumpkins, his favorite because the tall pumpkins allow good face carving. He also grows a variety of flat and round pumpkins for jack-o'-lanterns, two varieties of white pumpkins, and even a persimmon-colored pumpkin called Cinderella.

On October weekends, farm stands and farm markets are ablaze with masses of these pumpkins, and the farmers go to great lengths to make them marketable. The Big Rock, on M-43, paints the boulder that gives the farm its name as a jack-o'-lantern. It's an eye-catching display, even on fast-moving M-43.

Nearby, Darlene and Gene Rhodes go all out to sell their pumpkins. They'll attract your attention with their pumpkin mailbox, wear pumpkin-orange clothes when they greet you, show

Some farmers go all out when they make their pumpkin displays.

you the sales room in a pumpkin-orange barn, park their orange-painted car in front of their orange-trimmed garage with the pumpkin mural on the door, and do other subtle things to remind you that it's pumpkin time.

Jacki Droski brings her grandfather's pumpkins to the Fulton Street Farmers' Market. On her own farm, she raises blueberries, but she sells that crop to a processor so she can spend time making hundreds of witch hats for the fall pumpkins, which she paints and displays. We asked her if she used a special paint, perhaps an acrylic. She replied, "Of course. I use pumpkin paint." Topped with her witch hats, these whimsical pumpkin people that Jacki creates are worth going out of your way to buy.

Cathy Schaefer, who grows pumpkins on her farm in Sparta, also paints them to bring to market. She paints witch faces, as does Jacki Droski, but she also paints more traditionally styled jack-o'-lantern faces and "monster" faces. In addition, she makes pumpkin scarecrows. Cathy "just loves Halloween," she says, and her decorated pumpkins may well "like to live on your porch for the holiday."

It's no wonder that, with all the pumpkins, gourds, and Indian corn available, Michigan homeowners decorate their houses and porches to welcome the neighborhood trick-or-treaters. And on Halloween, whole blocks and whole towns go all out with Halloween parties. One street near our home closes to traffic and holds games and contests for the kids, including the venerable bobbing for apples. Homeowners play spooky music over loudspeakers and compete with elaborate decorations.

Halloween is a big celebration in Michigan, and it marks the end of the fall season for many of the farm stands and farm market farmers. It's a good time — and with luck we've stocked up enough for winter.

FALL RECIPES

Cream of Tomato Soup

SERVES FOUR

For years we've been buying tasty tomatoes (and other fruit and vegetables) from Arnold Groeneveld at the Fulton Street market. When we asked if he had a special recipe for his tomatoes, he told us this soup was wonderful. It originally came from one of the Moline Baptist Church cookbooks.

- 2 cups milk
- 2 scant tablespoons cornstarch
- ¼ cup cold water
- 2 cups strained tomatoes (juice)
  salt and pepper to taste
- 2 tablespoons margarine

Measure the milk into the top of a double boiler, then add the cornstarch dissolved in the cold water. Stir constantly over the boiling water until the mixture thickens. Have the tomato juice heating in a separate pan, and add slowly to the thickened milk mixture, stirring rapidly. (Warning: This may curdle if you try adding the milk to the tomato juice.) Add the salt, pepper, and margarine, and serve immediately.

Cabbage and Brown Rice Soup

SERVES FOUR

This is another recipe from our friend and herbalist Ray Kwapil. Ray loves to cook, and this makes an easy, quick supper, which has become one of our favorites. We like to serve it with a good crusty bread, cheese, and fall fruits, including apple wedges, pear slices, and grapes.

1 tablespoon vegetable oil
1 tablespoon butter or margarine
1 medium onion, sliced
2 cups cabbage, chopped
4½ cups beef broth or bouillon
1½ tablespoons soy sauce
½ cup brown rice or ¾ cup quick rice
salt and pepper to taste

Heat the oil and butter in a kettle and sauté the onion until limp. Add the cabbage and stir until it, too, is tender. Next add the broth and soy sauce and bring to a boil. Then add the rice, cover, and simmer for 30 minutes (20 minutes if you're using quick rice). If the soup is too thick at this point, add a little more water. Stir in the salt and pepper and serve.

Borscht (Beet Soup)

SERVES SIX TO EIGHT

Our neighbor, Nancy Holodnick, grew up in the thumb of the state, where they grow lots of sugar beets. She often serves this old family recipe to her family.

1 ham bone
3 quarts water
4 beets, cooked, skinned, and cubed
2 cups cabbage, coarsely shredded
1 onion, chopped
2-3 potatoes, cubed
2 carrots, sliced in rounds
3-4 sprigs fresh dill
sour cream and cream of tartar (optional)

Cook the ham bone in the water and remove the meat and bone, leaving the stock. Add all the remaining ingredients except the last two and bring to a boil. Simmer for 45 minutes. Serve hot, topped with a spoonful of sour cream and a dash of cream of tartar.

Joy's Marinated Vegetable Salad

SERVES EIGHT TO TEN

Our daughter loves to share recipes with us, and phones us from Massachusetts almost weekly with some new concoction. When we told her that our friends devoured this healthy dish at a potluck supper, she was pleased. She was even more pleased when we told her we were going to include it in this book.

- 1 small head cauliflower, in florets
- 1 bunch broccoli, in florets
- 1 pound carrots, sliced in rounds
- 1 small onion, thinly sliced in rings
- 4 ribs celery, sliced thin
- 1 small can pitted black olives
- ¼ cup Italian dressing
- ¼ cup Parmesan cheese

Blanch the cauliflower, broccoli, and carrots until crisp-tender. Add the other ingredients and toss. This is best served at room temperature.

Red Cabbage (Rotkohl)

SERVES SIX

Bill Seeger, a professor of foreign languages at Grand Valley State University, shares this favorite recipe, one he always made for the planning sessions of our Murder by the Book group, which presented annual "Mystery Days" at the Grand Rapids Public Library. (Some of those sessions got pretty wild, but that was never the fault of the red cabbage.)

Bill's family owns the Schnitzelbank Restaurant, Grand Rapids' oldest and best-known German restaurant, and their red cabbage remains a menu staple.

- 1 medium-to-large red cabbage (2½ to 3 pounds)
- 2 tablespoons sugar

2 teaspoons salt
⅔ cup red wine vinegar
2 tablespoons lard or vegetable oil
½ cup onion, chopped fine
2 medium cooking apples, peeled and cored,
  cut into ⅛-inch wedges
1 bay leaf
1 small onion, peeled
4-6 whole cloves
1 cup boiling water
3 tablespoons red wine

Wash the cabbage under cold water, remove the outer leaves, and cut the head lengthwise into quarters. Remove the core, and cut each quarter crosswise into strips as fine as possible. Put the cabbage in a large bowl and add the sugar, salt, and vinegar, tossing to mix thoroughly.

Heat the lard or oil in a large (4 to 5 quart) cooking pot over medium heat, and add the chopped onions and apples, stirring frequently until the apple slices are slightly browned (about five minutes). Add the cabbage, the bay leaf, and the whole onion, pierced with the cloves. Stir the mixture well, and then add the boiling water. Bring the contents of the pot to a boil over high heat, stirring occasionally, then turn the heat down to its lowest point. Cover and allow to simmer until the cabbage is tender (about 1½ to 2 hours), checking to make sure the cabbage remains moist.

When the cabbage is ready, hardly any liquid should be left in the pot (although if the mixture looks dry, add a tablespoon of boiling water). Remove the bay leaf and the whole onion, add the red wine, and stir. Serve in a heated bowl.

Authors' note: Bill says that this red cabbage goes very well with pot roasts such as sauerbraten, with beef rouladen, and with game such as rabbit and venison.

Cabbage in Sour Cream Sauce

SERVES FOUR TO SIX

Cabbage, except for coleslaw, is too often dismissed on the American scene, but Ray Kwapil, who shares this recipe with us, says, "Those of us with family roots in Middle Europe know that it's an exceedingly diverse vegetable. In something like vegetable soup, for example, it is critical. We've had this recipe around for years, so I don't know where it came from." But it definitely is "Middle European" in flavor.

- 2 tablespoons butter
- 1 small head cabbage, shredded
- 1 egg, beaten
- 1 cup sour cream
- 2 tablespoons sugar
- 3 tablespoons vinegar or lemon juice
  salt and pepper to taste

Melt the butter in a large skillet, then add the cabbage, stirring well. Cover tightly and cook until tender but not browned. Mix the other ingredients together and add to the cabbage over low heat. Simmer, but do not boil. When thoroughly heated, serve at once.

Glazed Apple Chicken

SERVES TWO

This chicken, glazed with a combination of apple wine and apple cider, is perfect for a late summer or fall dinner after a trip to the farmers' market.

- 2 tablespoons margarine
- 2 large chicken breasts, skinned and boned
- 1 teaspoon brown sugar
- 2 tablespoons Herman Jansen reinforced apple wine
- ¼ cup apple cider
- ¼ cup chicken broth

1 tablespoon margarine
2 small Empire apples, pitted and wedged
  dash of cinnamon

Melt the margarine in a no-stick skillet over medium heat, then add the chicken and brown. Sprinkle the brown sugar over the chicken and continue cooking until the sugar melts, about one more minute. Next pour the apple wine, apple cider, and chicken broth into the skillet and heat to boiling. Reduce heat and simmer until the chicken is done; remove the chicken to a platter and keep warm. Then turn up the heat under the skillet and quickly reduce the cider mixture to a glaze. While making the glaze, sauté the apple slices in a little margarine until they're softened and browned, then add a dash of cinnamon. Arrange the slices and the chicken breasts on plates, and pour the glaze over both.

Authors' note: If you substitute an apple brandy for the wine, try adding it before you add the cider and the broth. Pour the brandy over the chicken and flame it. The searing will keep the chicken juicy, and you'll still get the good apple taste.

Stir-Fried Chicken and Fall Vegetables

SERVES FOUR

We make this all the time. We vary the ingredients, sometimes adding green peppers, tomatoes, and cashews instead of the walnuts. Sometimes we just use vegetables, omit the nuts, and add a tablespoon of Hoisin sauce with the broth. Regardless of what we do, the proportions and order of ingredients always yield a delicious dish.

1 tablespoon vegetable oil
2 teaspoons soy sauce
1 teaspoon cornstarch
2 whole, skinless and boneless chicken breasts, cut in strips
½ cup chicken broth
½ teaspoon ground ginger
1 tablespoon soy sauce
2 teaspoons cornstarch

2 tablespoons vegetable oil
½ teaspoon dried red pepper flakes (or to taste)
1 medium onion, sliced lengthwise
2 cloves garlic, minced
1 small red pepper, sliced lengthwise
1 cup mushrooms, sliced
1 cup broccoli florets
¼ pound snow peas, trimmed and rinsed
½ cup walnuts, chopped

Mix the first tablespoon of oil with the 2 teaspoons of soy sauce and the single teaspoon of cornstarch and coat the chicken with it. Cover and refrigerate for thirty minutes. Then mix together the broth, the ginger, the single tablespoon of soy sauce, and the two teaspoons of cornstarch and set aside.

In a wok or heavy skillet, heat the oil and stir-fry the coated chicken until it's no longer pink. Add the dried red pepper and sauté a minute or two longer. Remove the chicken from the skillet and stir-fry the onion, garlic, and red pepper slices until tender. Then add the mushrooms, the broccoli, and the snow peas, and stir-fry until tender. Now return the chicken to the skillet, add the broth mixture, and cook until it thickens, stirring constantly.

Add the walnuts, stir, and serve immediately with a side dish of rice.

Authors' note: We like this dish quite spicy, but it's still tasty if you omit or reduce the amount of dried red pepper.

Spinach Lasagna

SERVES SIX

Roberta Jacobson of Leelanau Cellars suggested that we share this vegetarian fall meal, which she's included in her recipe collection entitled "A Taste of Northern Michigan."

1 box (1 pound) lasagna noodles
2 tablespoons oil
1 medium onion, chopped

1 large garlic bud, minced
  1 pound fresh tomatoes, chopped,
      or 1 16-ounce can tomatoes, chopped
  1 6-ounce can tomato paste
  ½ cup Leelanau Cellars Autumn Harvest or Baco Noir wine
  1 teaspoon sugar
  1 teaspoon salt
  ½ teaspoon oregano
  ½ teaspoon dried basil, or 1 tablespoon fresh basil, chopped
  2 packages frozen chopped spinach, thawed and drained
  1 egg, beaten
  1 16-ounce container ricotta or cottage cheese
  ¼ cup Parmesan cheese
12-16 ounces mozzarella cheese, grated or sliced

Cook the noodles according to package directions, drain, rinse, and set aside. Sauté the onion and garlic in the oil until tender. Add the chopped tomatoes, tomato paste, and wine. Next stir in the sugar, salt, oregano, and basil. Simmer for 15 to 20 minutes. In a bowl, put the spinach, beaten egg, ricotta, and Parmesan cheese, and stir until mixed.

   In a greased 9 × 13-inch glass pan, put a layer of cooked noodles. Follow with one-third the tomato sauce, half the spinach mixture, and one-third the mozzarella. Layer once more, and end with noodles, sauce, and mozzarella. Bake, uncovered, at 350° for 35 to 45 minutes.

Beef Stew Leelanau

SERVES SIX

This is another recipe from Roberta Jacobson's collection called "A Taste of Northern Michigan." It's a classic stew.

  1½ pounds beef chuck, cut in cubes
  1 tablespoon shortening
  1 clove garlic, minced
  1 medium onion, chopped

        ½ teaspoon salt
        ¼ teaspoon pepper
        1 can tomato soup, undiluted
        ¼ cup water
        ¾ cup Leelanau Cellars Autumn Harvest wine
        ¼ teaspoon dried basil
        ¼ teaspoon thyme
        3 medium carrots, sliced
      1½ cups celery, sliced
        4 medium potatoes, pared and sliced

Brown the beef in the shortening. Next, add the garlic and onion and sauté until tender. Add the salt and pepper, then stir in the tomato soup, water, and wine. Cover and simmer for 30 minutes. Then add the basil, thyme, and vegetables, and simmer for two hours or until tender.

Authors' note: Roberta Jacobson says this stew can be made the day before, and may even be better served the next day.

The Pumpkin Is the Casserole

SERVES SIX

Darlene and Gene Rhodes, who operate a farm on M-43, west of Kalamazoo, call themselves "the Pumpkin People." Every year Darlene publishes a pumpkin-orange–covered booklet of pumpkin and squash recipes. This recipe appears in her third edition, and you can get a free copy when you visit the Rhodes' farm. It seemed like a natural to us for a Halloween supper, and it was. Not only did it taste good, but the pumpkin turned a beautiful terra-cotta color, looking almost ceramic and becoming a smashing centerpiece as well as the main course.

        1 5-6 pound round pumpkin
        ½ teaspoon salt
        ¼ teaspoon pepper
        ¼ cup butter
        1 medium onion, minced
        1 clove garlic, minced

    1 green pepper, minced
    1 pound ground beef
    ½ teaspoon thyme
    3 tomatoes, peeled and quartered
    1 cup beef broth or bouillon
    2 tablespoons dry white wine
 1½ cups cooked rice
    ½ cup cheddar cheese, grated

Remove the lid from the pumpkin and save, then scoop out the seeds and stringy matter. Score the inside of the pumpkin several times and rub it with salt and pepper. Place the pumpkin upside down in a large shallow pan filled with ¼ inch of water. Place the lid in the pan alongside the pumpkin. Bake in a 350° oven for one hour, or until tender. Drain and set aside.

In a skillet, melt the butter and sauté the onion, garlic, and green pepper. Add the ground beef and thyme, and simmer until the meat is browned. Next add the tomatoes, broth, and wine, and cook until the liquid is substantially reduced. Stir in the cooked rice and mix thoroughly.

Stuff the pumpkin with this mixture, top with the cheese, and return to the oven until the cheese is melted. Replace the lid until serving, and then serve from the pumpkin. The pumpkin pulp should be scooped out and served with the stuffing.

Authors' note: This recipe should serve six, but when we tried it, four hungry adults managed to devour it — although we couldn't move for the rest of the evening.

Laurie's Pumpkin Stew

MAKES TWELVE CUPS

Our niece, Laurie Lesser Hodgson, says this is the best ever, with a "very interesting combination of ingredients." Laurie is a professional artist and designer, so this is also a pretty dish.

    1 5-6 pound pumpkin
      butter

    salt and pepper
1   pound hamburger
2   medium onions, chopped
1   cup green pepper, chopped
2   cups corn
2   cups green beans, sliced
2   fresh peaches, diced
1   cup cooked chicken, diced
1   cup sunflower seeds

Cut out the lid of the pumpkin jack-o'-lantern style and scoop out the seeds and stringy matter. Rub the inside of the pumpkin with the butter, salt, and pepper. Bake without the lid at 350° for 40 to 45 minutes. Keep checking to see if water is accumulating in the pumpkin, and remove it if it is. (Note: This is the way Laurie does it, but if you cook the pumpkin upside down, as Darlene Rhodes suggests, you'll have no problem with water accumulating in the pumpkin.)

While the pumpkin is cooking, sauté the hamburger, onions, and green pepper. Combine this mixture with the corn, green beans, peaches, chicken, and sunflower seeds. Cook for one hour, adding water to keep the mixture moist.

Fill the warm pumpkin with this stew, and serve from the pumpkin, scooping out the pulp and serving it alongside the stew.

Microwave Baked Apple

SERVES ONE

Diane Sietsema, of Sietsema Orchards and Cider Mill in Grand Rapids, says, "Try apples in your microwave. Creating an almost instant baked apple has never been easier."

1   medium to large baking apple
1   tablespoon brown sugar
1½   teaspoons margarine, softened
     dash of cinnamon

Core the apple and slice the skin around the circumference half an inch from the top. Cream together the brown sugar, margarine, and cinnamon. Fill the center of the apple with this mixture and place it in a small microwave-safe dish. Cover with waxed paper and microwave on full power for two to three minutes, rotating the dish halfway through the cooking time. Test the apple with a fork for tenderness and serve warm or cold.

Authors' note: Don't make just one!

Caramel Apple Pie

SERVES EIGHT

We saw Diane Sietsema, of Sietsema Orchards and Cider Mill, cook this on TV. It looked so good we asked for the recipe.

    5 cups Jonathan, Rome, or Gala apples, unpeeled and cut in
      ½-inch cubes
    1 tablespoon lemon juice
    ½ cup flour
    1 cup caramel ice-cream topping
    1 pie crust
    1 package caramel apple wraps
    ½ cup pecan pieces, chopped

Mix together the chopped apples, lemon juice, flour, and caramel topping. Put half the mixture in the pie crust and layer with two sheets of caramel apple wraps. Then put in the remaining mixture and top with two more wraps. Sprinkle with the chopped pecans and bake at 375° for 45 minutes.

Authors' note: For variety, Diane suggests, add some chocolate chips or shredded coconut.

Mary Bethel Robinette's Apple Slices

SERVES FIFTEEN TO EIGHTEEN

Mary Bethel Robinette, of Robinette's Orchards on Four Mile Road in Grand Rapids, says that this is her favorite apple recipe for feeding a crowd. She serves it with hot apple cider, and we include her recipe for that, too.

- 4 cups flour
- 2 teaspoons salt
- 2 teaspoons sugar
- 2 cups shortening
- 2 egg yolks and milk to equal ⅔ cup
- 6-7 cups apples, peeled and sliced
- 1 cup sugar
- 1 teaspoon cinnamon
- ½ teaspoon nutmeg
- dash mace
- butter
- 2 tablespoons milk
- 1 cup powdered sugar

Mix together the flour, salt, and sugar, and cut the shortening into it. Add the egg yolk/milk mixture and stir until you have a very moist dough. Chill the dough for about an hour, then roll out half of it and line a jelly-roll pan with it (dough is very tender). Mix the apples with the sugar, cinnamon, and nutmeg, and fill the dough with this mixture, then dot with butter. Roll out the remaining dough to cover the pan. Make small slits in the dough with a knife and bake at 400° for 10 minutes. Then reduce the temperature to 375° and continue baking for about 30 minutes or until the crust is brown. While the pie is still warm, glaze with a mixture of milk and powdered sugar.

Hot Apple Cider

SERVES TWENTY

  1 gallon cider
  2 tablespoons honey
12 whole cloves
  2 sticks cinnamon

Pour the cider into a big pot and add the spices. (You can put the spices in a tea ball or a twist of cheesecloth and then remove that when the cider's hot.) Simmer until hot, but do not boil.

Raw Apple Cake

SERVES EIGHT

Leona Van Koevering of Hudsonville always seems delighted whenever we stop at her booth at the Fulton Street Farmers' Market. She's always smiling, and always has something particularly fine that day. On one cold fall day, when it was the apples that pleased her the most, she took the time to jot down this especially fine recipe for us to share.

    CAKE:
2 cups sugar
1 cup butter
4 eggs, beaten
3 cups flour
1 teaspoon ground cloves
2 teaspoons cinnamon
1 teaspoon nutmeg
2 teaspoons baking soda
⅛ teaspoon salt
1 cup cold coffee
3 cups apples, peeled and sliced
1 cup raisins
1 cup walnuts, chopped

TOPPING:

2 tablespoons melted butter
3 tablespoons cream
½ cup brown sugar
½ cup coconut, shredded

Cream the sugar and butter, then add in the beaten eggs. Mix all the dry ingredients together and add gradually to the creamed mixture, alternating with the coffee. Then add the apples, raisins, and nuts, and mix well. Bake in a greased 9 × 13-inch glass pan at 350° for one hour. Mix together the ingredients for the topping and spread on the cake. Put the cake under the broiler until the topping browns. Serve warm.

Knobby Apple Cake

SERVES EIGHT

Most of the young people who help her sell fruit at the Fulton Street Farmers' Market call her Grandma Tanis, and now so do many of her regular customers. She's there rain or shine, and she'll help you pick out perfect fruit while offering you tastes of what's best that day. She says this recipe may have come originally from the Farm Bureau Women of Michigan.

2 tablespoons butter
½ cup white sugar
½ cup brown sugar
1 egg
1 teaspoon vanilla
3 cups apples, peeled and finely diced
1 cup flour
½ teaspoon salt
1 teaspoon baking soda
½ teaspoon cinnamon
½ teaspoon nutmeg
½ cup nut meats, chopped

Cream the butter and sugar, then beat in the egg and vanilla. Fold in the diced apples. Next mix the dry ingredients together and fold into the apple mixture. Add the nuts and mix well. Pour into a greased 9 × 13-inch glass pan and bake at 350° for 40 minutes.

Baked Pears

SERVES FOUR

This is a very easy dessert, and a favorite of our kids. We often serve it with a pasta dinner.

    4 ripe pears
    4 tablespoons dry white wine
    ¼ cup apricot preserves, forced through a sieve
    ½ cup macaroon crumbs (we like to use Italian
         amaretto biscotti)
    3 tablespoons butter, cut into pea-sized dots

Preheat the oven to 400°. Peel, quarter, and core the pears, then cut into lengthwise slices about ⅜-inch thick. Arrange in overlapping layers in a 9 x 13-inch greased glass baking dish. Beat the wine and apricot preserves together and pour over the pear slices. Then sprinkle with macaroon crumbs and distribute the butter over the surface. Bake in the middle of the oven for 20 to 30 minutes, or until the top has browned lightly. Serve warm or cold.

Apple Bread

MAKES ONE LARGE LOAF

Marge Geukes, of the Fulton Street Farmers' Market, gave us this recipe to use with a variety of fruits. Marge, her husband, John, and their cute little girls — who are now all grown-up, beautiful ladies — have been selling produce at the market for years. And it's great fun for us to hear the second-generation farm women sound just like their parents as they help one customer pick a perfect ripe cantaloupe and tell another customer just how to cook the apples for sauce.

BREAD:

½ cup margarine
¾ cup sugar
2 eggs
⅓ cup sour milk
1 teaspoon vanilla
2 cups flour
1 teaspoon baking soda
2 cups apples, peeled and shredded, *or*
2 cups rhubarb, chopped, *or*
2 cups blueberries, *or*
2 cups raspberries

Authors' note: Marge uses ½ cup sour milk in the rhubarb and berry breads.

TOPPING (optional):

2 tablespoons margarine
2 tablespoons sugar
2 tablespoons flour
½ teaspoon cinnamon

Cream the margarine, sugar, and eggs together. Mix the remaining ingredients into the creamed mixture, adding the fruit last. Pour into a greased loaf pan. Mix the topping ingredients together and spread on the loaf before baking. Bake at 350° for one hour.

Applesauce

MAKES TWO QUARTS

This is sort of a composite of many recipes. It's best when made with several kinds of apples, but most should be red to give the sauce that lovely pink color.

6 pounds apples, cored and cut in eighths
3 tablespoons sugar, or to taste
½ cup water

In a heavy pot, combine the apples, sugar, and water. Cook over low heat, covered, until the apples are very tender, about twenty minutes. Uncover and let cool. Then pass the apples through a food mill or coarse sieve. Taste and adjust the sugar. Add a dash of nutmeg or cinnamon for variety.

Grandma's Applesauce

Virginia Saur of Saur Corners Farm shares this recipe for applesauce. Her daughter, Mary Bayer, first called it to our attention when she heard we were writing this book, and she insists it's the best applesauce recipe ever!

Peel, core, and slice any firm apples and put in a heavy pot. Add sugar to taste and a scant amount of water to prevent scorching. Simmer slowly until the apples are tender and glazed over. Mash, then add a couple of teaspoonsful of red-hot cinnamon candies and stir to melt. This adds both a pink color and a cinnamon flavor!

Authors' note: When we tried this recipe, we used about ten apples, and we ended up with about a quart of applesauce.

Pumpkin-Applesauce Tea Bread

MAKES TWO LOAVES

This is another recipe from Darlene Rhodes of "the Pumpkin People." It is published in her booklet called "Pumpkin and Winter Squash Recipes, Third Edition," which may be obtained at no charge at the Rhodes' farm on M-43.

    2 cups sugar
    ⅓ cup molasses
    1 cup pumpkin, cooked
    1 cup applesauce
    ⅔ cup vegetable oil

     3 eggs
   ⅓ cup milk
3⅔ cups flour
1½ teaspoons baking soda
     2 teaspoons cinnamon
     1 teaspoon nutmeg
     1 teaspoon vanilla
     1 cup nuts, chopped
     1 cup raisins or chopped dates

Put sugar, molasses, pumpkin, applesauce, oil, eggs, and milk in a large bowl and mix at medium speed until well blended. Sift the dry ingredients together and add to the mixture, blending thoroughly. Then add the vanilla, nuts, and raisins or dates, mixing well with a spoon. Pour into two well-greased 9 × 5-inch loaf pans and bake at 350° for one hour. Cool on wire racks for ten minutes, then remove from the pans. Wrap in foil and store overnight.

Authors' note: Darlene offers this suggestion: "Try this recipe in muffin tins also. When ready to serve, take out of foil wrap and place on a paper doily on a little saucer. Elegant!"

Zucchini Bread

MAKES ONE BUNDT-SIZE LOAF

Jeanne N. Sarna, C.H.E., the Director of the Tower Test Kitchen of the Detroit Free Press, *sent us her own recipe for zucchini bread.*

     floured baking spray or 1 tablespoon shortening
     and 1 tablespoon flour
     3 cups flour
     1 teaspoon cinnamon
     1 teaspoon salt
     1 teaspoon baking soda
     1 teaspoon baking powder
     2 cups sugar
     3 large eggs, beaten
     1 cup vegetable oil

2 teaspoons vanilla
1 cup coconut, shredded
1½ cups nuts, chopped
3 cups zucchini, washed, ends removed, and shredded

Preheat oven to 325°. Spray a bundt pan with floured baking spray or grease and dust with flour. In a large bowl, sift together the flour, cinnamon, salt, baking soda, and baking powder. Set aside. In a second large bowl, beat together the sugar, eggs, oil, vanilla, coconut, nuts, and zucchini. Then beat the flour mixture into the egg mixture. Pour into the prepared bundt pan and bake for 1½ hours, or until a wooden pick or bamboo skewer inserted in the bread comes out clean.

WINTER

REGARDLESS OF THE SOLSTICE, WINTER IN MICHIGAN begins in November. The grass has turned a gray brown, and so have the few leaves still hanging on trees. Skies become uniformly gray, temperatures routinely flirt with freezing, and eventually there is snow. Michigan in winter is brown, gray, and white.

The Fulton Street market in winter:
the last vestiges of the growing season

But farm markets are still islets of color in the Michigan landscape, with most of the regular farmers bringing produce to market until shortly after the first hard frost. They will have picked and stored enough fruits and vegetables to last a few weeks after that frost. They'll bring their tomatoes and their potatoes. They'll bring broccoli, cauliflower, and cabbage. And they'll enhance these homegrown wares with fruits and vegetables from Southern states that they've purchased from wholesale markets.

Farmers will bring their own homegrown apples, particularly the hearty apples of late fall like Romes and Baldwins. In 1992, Raymond Richards was the last of the apple farmers to come to the Fulton Street Farmers' Market. An unusually cool and slow growing year meant that Ray was able to pick his Rome and Baldwin apples in late November at his South Haven orchard. Usually, he shows at Holland, but after that market closed, he brought his fruit to Fulton Street — the Romes and Baldwins and some Jonathans he had stored. By then, the other farmers were selling only Christmas trees and greens.

Produce Storage

Storage of fruits and vegetables for winter use deserves some comment, and it's a tricky process. Few of us have root cellars anymore, but we all have spots in our houses where we have tried to store produce. Large farms have cold-storage rooms where apples can be kept at around 40 degrees. That's an almost perfect temperature. Much colder, and there would be the danger of frost. Much warmer, and the apples wouldn't keep well.

Darlene Rhodes warns that you also have to be careful about what you store together. She cautions that you should never store apples and squash together, for example, because the squash won't keep. Fruits and vegetables emit gases, including those odors that make you think an apple smells like an apple, and in this instance that has a negative effect on the squash.

Winter squash may be stored a good long time, according to Darlene, if it's kept at about 50 degrees. Never refrigerate it, and make sure there's room for air circulation around the vegetables. Too little moisture is bad, but so is too much, so she wraps the vegetables in newspaper to avoid excessive moisture. She also freezes squash so she's sure to have enough to last until the next crop comes in.

Darlene suggests that you bake squash whole, after poking

A farmer sells the last of his apple crop on a wintry day at market.

holes in the skin to prevent them from exploding in the oven. With a tough squash, she uses a screwdriver to penetrate the shell.

Dried flowers and Indian corn are another early winter attraction at Michigan farm markets and stands, as are cut, fresh flowers, notably mums. Most of these farm products are available in the fall, but another peak market time is when shoppers are thinking about decorating their homes for the winter holidays.

Moser's Flower Barn in Spring Lake and Flowers of the Field in Grand Rapids are huge shops specializing in dried flowers and other farm products, and they have become wonderlands of decorating inspiration, particularly for the holidays. We discovered Moser's first, but because of distance we've gotten to know Flowers of the Field better.

At that shop, big bunches of statice in shades of purple, yellow, white, and blue might be what you first decide to buy. The Andres devote a field of five acres to supply the 3,000 to 4,000

Dried Flowers

handpicked bunches that they sell at their store. They even pick from one special row of plants with mauve, pink, and blue blossoms. They call those bunches of statice "Grandma Bolt," because Norma Andre's grandmother always wore those colors.

Then you might buy some strawflowers in shades of orange and yellow. The beautiful displays arranged by the Andres show how miniature pumpkins and gourds, as well as Indian corn and dried grains, can grace a Thanksgiving table. We find it refreshing that the Andres love decorating for Thanksgiving, and don't put out Christmas greens and ornaments until the first holiday is over. When you remember that mall stores may begin the Christmas season before Halloween, we think you'll appreciate the Andres' forbearance and being able to "glean" numerous ideas for a festive Thanksgiving at their shop.

Turkey

A further word about Thanksgiving. When you're on the back roads near Marshall, try and stop at Cornwell's Turkeyville U.S.A.

A bright fan of Michigan holly makes a festive Christmas decoration.

While this can't really be considered a farm stand, it was once only a turkey farm, and now it's the largest turkey specialty restaurant in the country, serving its own turkey. Cornwell's is decorated with antiques and country-style decorations, some of which you can buy in its "Country Junction," a large gift shop. It holds flea markets, antique shows, and arts-and-crafts shows. It also has a dinner theatre that offers several different shows a year, a pumpkin-carving contest, and a Christmas open house.

In Cornwell's restaurant, you can order turkey meals ranging from "Sloppy Toms" to full turkey dinners, and you can take home many of the menu items. But you can't do that on Thanksgiving. It's closed for the holiday.

The major winter farm business in Michigan is, of course, the sale of Christmas trees. Over five million trees are harvested each year in Michigan, and there are dozens of varieties.

Christmas Trees and Greens

The hearty farmers who bring their trees to the municipal farm markets are, by and large, not the same farmers who come all year, although at the Fulton Street market, bundled-up Betty Nitz and Leona Van Koevering were selling bunches of red-berried Michigan holly and Christmas greens late in November, and trying to stay warm near space heaters.

The trees and greens are fresh at the market, not cut weeks or even months before, and the families who know this, who often bring their very young children, do crowd the market to make their selections.

Be forewarned: the Christmas-tree sale at the farm market is frigid. The red cheeks of the children mean they're cold, and you will be too — there's no colder place to go. It defies the laws of physics. You start out on a sunny morning with moderate temperatures, and by the time you reach the market, it's cold, wet, and gray. So wear layers of clothes — you can't wear too many — and have the hot chocolate ready when you bring the tree home.

Cut-your-own-tree farms surround all the large cities of Michigan, and many of those farms provide free hot chocolate and coffee for everybody who comes.

Tree Farms

In Ingham County, Sno-cap Tree Farm offers both cut and live trees, with a transplanting service available. Skyhorse Station near Brighton and Thornhollow Tree Farm in Wayne County both offer cut-your-own spruces and pines.

Part of the season's charm: a cut-your-own Christmas tree

So from Detroit to the Indiana border and points north, you can cut your own tree and know there is none fresher to be had. And you'll have fun doing it. Pinecrest Farms, near Galen in southwest Michigan, is a cold spot that's warm and friendly. It has thousands of Scotch pines to choose from, offers haywagon rides, has an indoor showroom with precut trees (it's warmer in there), and offers hot chocolate and coffee. Jollay Orchards in Coloma also offers hayrides and sells hot cider and warm caramel apples to tree-cutters. Runyan's Country Tree Farm in Genesee County has hot cider and doughnuts, and in addition to cut-your-own trees offers live, potted spruce and pine trees. Also in Genesee County is Trim Pines Farm, which has live trees and a horse-drawn haywagon to take you to the fields.

We went to the Hart Farm, primarily because it's close to Grand Rapids. It's a no-frills Christmas-tree operation that Tom

Hart says was "originally his grandmother's dairy farm." Tom says his family has been planting and selling trees for fifty years.

They started with a planting of 2,000 Austrian pines, and now grow eleven varieties. We asked Tom how they started, and he explained: "When my parents decided to get out of the dairy business, much of the land was too hilly for the tractor and plowing. Trees make a good crop on that kind of land."

The Hart Farm has beautiful trees, planted far apart on the rolling ground so that they develop pleasing shapes. It seemed to us that many were certainly nice enough to be sold as nursery stock, but Tom explained the problem with trying to serve two markets: "Digging trees leaves holes, which is incompatible with a safe cut-your-own operation." After fifty years, that's what the Harts know how to do best.

And they have all they can handle just dealing with Christmas trees and greens. They'll listen to your needs and tell you which of the varieties come closest to matching your requirements, then they'll tell you where the best ones are growing. They'll supply saws for you to cut down your tree. And when you've got it, they'll shake it free of loose needles and bale it for you. They also cut a stock of trees daily for those customers who don't want to cut their own. And they maintain a shop filled with homemade wreaths, boughs, and evergreen ropes to meet your additional decorating needs. In short, what they do best is make it easy for you to buy a high-quality tree and decorations. What more do you need at Christmas?

WINTER RECIPES

Six-Layer Dinner

SERVES EIGHT

Grandma Tanis of Tanis Orchards on Fruit Ridge in Grand Rapids gave us one of her favorite old recipes, originally from the Farm Bureau Women of Michigan. Like many winter farm recipes, this uses root vegetables and canned vegetables, either those the farmer has put up or store-bought commercial products.

2-3	potatoes, sliced
¼	cup rice, uncooked
2	pounds lean ground beef, browned
3	small onions, chopped
2	green peppers, sliced
1	large can tomatoes
	salt and pepper to taste

Grease the bottom of a large glass baking dish, then cover with the potato slices and season lightly. Then layer the uncooked rice, meat, onions, and peppers in that order, seasoning each layer. Pour the tomatoes over all. Bake at 325° for 1½ to 2 hours.

Chicken Lasagna

SERVES SIX

We first met Brenda Heffron of Heffron Farms when another farmer told us we shouldn't miss visiting there during the Kent Harvest Trail celebration. He told us the Heffrons were such nice people, and that they had arranged wagon tours of their beef-cattle farm. He was right. But he didn't warn us that Brenda would be leading a purple cow around to greet children. We also discovered that, in addition to beef,

Heffron Farms offers frozen turkey and chicken parts. This is one of Brenda's chicken recipes.

½ cup green pepper, chopped
½ cup onion, chopped
3 tablespoons butter
1 can cream of chicken soup
⅓ cup milk
1 6-ounce can sliced mushrooms, drained
¼ cup pimento, chopped
½ teaspoon dried sweet basil
8 ounces lasagna noodles, cooked according to
   package directions
1½ cups creamed cottage cheese
3 cups cooked chicken, diced
2 cups Parmesan cheese, grated

Sauté the green pepper and onion in the butter. Stir in the soup, milk, mushrooms, pimento, and basil. Place half the noodles in a 13 × 9 × 2-inch greased glass baking dish, and cover with half the mushroom mixture, cottage cheese, chicken, and Parmesan cheese. Repeat the layers. Then bake at 350°, covered, for 45 minutes. Let stand for five minutes before serving.

Easy Crock-Pot Round Steak

SERVES SIX

Brenda Heffron of Heffron Farms sent us this recipe, good to prepare on a busy winter day.

2 pounds round steak, cut in strips
2 tablespoons oil
1 large onion, sliced
1 can cream of mushroom soup
1 can cream of celery soup
1 soupcan water
   salt and pepper to taste

Pan-fry the meat in the oil until browned, then transfer to the Crock-Pot. Sauté the onion in the oil and add to the pot. Then add the mushroom soup, celery soup, and water, seasoning with salt and pepper. Cook on low heat in the Crock-Pot for 6 to 8 hours. Serve over warm noodles or potatoes.

Authors' note: You can thicken the sauce after cooking by adding two tablespoons of cornstarch.

Traverse Bay Chicken

SERVES FOUR TO SIX

This is another fine recipe from Roberta Jacobson's collection called "A Taste of Northern Michigan." She uses her Leelanau Cellars Renaissance wine in the preparation, but suggests that the dish might also be served with their Spring Splendor or Winter White wine.

3-4 pounds chicken, cut up
¼ cup olive oil
2 medium onions, diced
2 cloves garlic, minced
1 16-ounce can tomatoes
1 8-ounce can tomato sauce
1 teaspoon salt
¼ teaspoon pepper
1 teaspoon oregano or basil
1-2 bay leaves
½ cup Leelanau Cellars Renaissance wine

In a skillet, brown the chicken in the olive oil, then remove. Next add the onions and garlic and sauté until tender. Return the chicken to the skillet and add all the remaining ingredients except the wine. Cover and simmer for 45 minutes. Then add the wine and cook uncovered, turning the chicken occasionally, for twenty minutes, or until the meat is tender. Remove the bay leaves before serving.

Italian Stuffed Spaghetti Squash

SERVES TWO

Spaghetti squash is fun food because the cooked flesh forms spaghetti-like strands that can be eaten almost like pasta. This recipe is another from Darlene Rhodes of "the Pumpkin People." It's easy to prepare and delicious.

1 medium spaghetti squash
1 tablespoon vegetable oil
½ cup onion, chopped
¼ cup celery, chopped
1 clove garlic, minced
½ pound ground beef
½ cup mushrooms, diced
⅓ cup rice, cooked
½ cup canned tomatoes
1 tablespoon fresh parsley, chopped
1 teaspoon oregano
¼ teaspoon pepper
½ teaspoon salt
¼ cup mozzarella cheese, shredded

Cut the squash in half, lengthwise, and remove the seeds. Place the halves cut side down in a baking pan filled with half an inch of water. Bake in a 350° oven for 30 minutes. In a large skillet, heat the vegetable oil and sauté the onion, celery, and garlic until soft. Add the ground beef and brown, then drain off the fat. Stir in the remaining ingredients except for the cheese and simmer for five minutes. Then turn the squash over and stuff with the filling. Sprinkle the halves with the cheese and bake for an additional thirty minutes.

Roast Turkey with Cherry Sauce

In the Traverse City area, cooks feverishly find new and better uses for cherries. This recipe from Debbie Simpson of Good Harbor Vineyards makes the traditional turkey a little more special.

    1 roast turkey, cooked on a Weber-type grill or
      oven-roasted in winter

    CHERRY SAUCE:
1½ tablespoons cornstarch
  4 tablespoons sugar
 ¼ teaspoon salt
 ¼ tablespoon dry mustard
 ¼ tablespoon ginger
 ½ cup Good Harbor Cherry wine
  1 tablespoon grated orange rind
 ½ cup orange juice
 ¼ cup currant jelly
  1 pound tart cherries, pitted (water pack if canned)
  2 tablespoons brandy

In a saucepan, combine the cornstarch, sugar, salt, dry mustard, and ginger. Add the cherry wine, orange rind, orange juice, and currant jelly. Cook over medium heat, stirring constantly, until thickened. Add the drained cherries and brandy before serving. Debbie suggests that you serve either their Birch White or Seyval Blanc wine with the roast turkey and cherry sauce.

American Spoon Holiday Stuffing

YIELDS ENOUGH STUFFING FOR AN 18-POUND TURKEY

Justin Rashid, founder of American Spoon, shares the recipe for this festive stuffing, which uses dried Montmorency cherries. American Spoon reports that "since we introduced these chewy ruby red jewels, they have become prized by chefs and cherry lovers all over the country."

        6 ounces American Spoon Dried Red Tart Cherries
        1 cup Madeira wine
       14 slices day-old homemade-style white bread, toasted
           and torn into small pieces (about 8 cups)
      1½ cups pecan meats, toasted
        ½ cup sweet butter
        1 cup onion, chopped
        1 cup celery, chopped
        ½ cup shallots, chopped
        3 crisp apples, coarsely chopped
        ½ cup golden raisins
        ½ cup flat-leafed parsley, chopped
        2 teaspoons dried tarragon, crumbled
        1 teaspoon dried thyme
    10-12 sage leaves, crumbled
        1 teaspoon salt, or to taste
        1 teaspoon freshly ground pepper, or to taste

Place the cherries in a bowl with the Madeira and soak for several hours or overnight. In a large bowl, combine the bread pieces with the toasted pecans. Drain the cherries, reserving the Madeira, and add them to the bread mixture. In a skillet, melt the butter and sauté the onion, celery, and shallots until the vegetables are softened. Add to the bread mixture. Then add the remaining ingredients and the reserved Madeira and toss the stuffing well.

Authors' note: Justin Rashid says that this stuffing is also a delicious accompaniment to roast goose, roast duck, and crown roast of pork.

Potato Puree with Parsley and Garlic

SERVES SIX

When we first proposed this book to William B. Eerdmans Publishing Company, Sam Eerdmans volunteered to taste every recipe in the book. We know he's tasted this one, since he forwarded it on to us from his friend, Andre Strong, of Blue Hill, Maine. (Sam serves as Sales Manager for the firm, but we don't suppose including a recipe from

Maine will enhance sales of this book in that state. On the other hand . . .)

2 pounds potatoes, preferably a yellow potato such as Yukon Gold
1 tablespoon salt
⅓ cup extra-virgin olive oil
4 large garlic cloves, peeled and crushed
1 cup (or more) flat-leaf parsley, stems removed
  salt and pepper to taste
1 cup scalding milk

Peel the potatoes and cut them into ½-inch-wide slices. Cover with cold water in a pot, add the tablespoon of salt, and bring to a boil. Cook until done (about thirty minutes), testing with a fork. Put the oil and garlic in a heavy-bottomed saucepan and heat very slowly for ten minutes. Cool.

Put the parsley in the bowl of a food processor fitted with a steel blade and strain the garlic oil in with the parsley, discarding the garlic. Season liberally with salt and pepper and process for two to three minutes, until a thin puree is formed. Add more parsley if it appears too thin.

Drain the potatoes and put them through a ricer or food mill. Add the puree and whip with a fork until blended. Add the scalded milk to moisten. Keep warm until ready to serve.

Potato Pancake

SERVES FOUR

We often stop for lunch or dinner at Hermann's European Café, an oasis for travelers right on U.S. 131 in downtown Cadillac. Viennese master chef Hermann Suhs does prepare European dishes, including the renowned pastries of his native Austria, but he has traveled around the world as a chef, so he also prepares food in Hawaiian, Caribbean, and even Thai style. This dish, however, is one that his great-grandmother made and served with homemade applesauce and sour cream. It's included in Cooking with Chef Hermann, *his 1991 cookbook, in which* he says, "She made the best Kartoffer Puffer by adding garlic. This is a poor man's Sunday brunch where one does not mind being poor."

    6 raw potatoes, peeled and chopped extremely fine
    2 eggs
    1 tablespoon parsley, chopped
    1 teaspoon salt
    2 cups heavy cream
    ½ cup flour

Mix all ingredients well. Adjust the consistency by adding more cream or flour, if necessary. Pour into a slightly greased hot skillet, and brown on both sides.

Cranberry-filled Acorn Squash

SERVES FOUR

This is a pretty, festive vegetable dish from the booklet printed up by Darlene Rhodes called "Pumpkin and Winter Squash Recipes, Third Edition."

    2 acorn squash
    3 cups cranberries
    ¾ cup apple juice, divided
    ¾ cup sugar
    ¼ teaspoon cloves
    ½ teaspoon nutmeg
    2 teaspoons cornstarch
    2 tablespoons walnuts, chopped

Pierce the rind of the squash and bake or microwave them, whole, until they're soft to the touch. Set aside. Combine the cranberries, ½ cup of the apple juice, the sugar, cloves, and nutmeg. Cook over low heat, stirring occasionally, until the cranberry skins "pop." Combine the remaining apple juice with the cornstarch, mixing well. Gradually stir this into the cranberry mixture and heat until just thickened.

Cut the squash in half, remove the seeds, and spoon the cranberry mixture into the squash shells. Sprinkle with the walnuts and place in the oven or microwave to heat thoroughly.

Harvard Beets

SERVES FOUR

Deanna House says that this is a wonderful dish and that this recipe, originally published in her More House Specialties *cookbook, must be included. She tells us that beets in a sweet-sour sauce have long been a popular and traditional dish in New England.*

- 1 tablespoon cornstarch
- 2 tablespoons sugar
- ¼ teaspoon salt
- 1 can (16 ounces) diced beets, drained, with the juice reserved
- ½ cup beet juice with water added to make the measure
- ¼ cup vinegar

In a one-quart, microwave-safe casserole, blend the cornstarch, sugar, and salt. Stir in the beet juice and vinegar. Microwave on full power for 2 to 4 minutes, stirring every minute, until thickened. Then add the beets and microwave on full power for 3 to 4 minutes until hot, stirring once.

Cherry Cobbler

SERVES FOUR

This recipe comes from Amon Orchards, north of Traverse City, where the pumpkins appear to grow in trees. It is Grandma Amon's secret recipe, in which "the secret ingredient, of course, is grandma's love!"

- ¼ cup butter or margarine
- ½ cup flour
- ¼ cup sugar

- 1 teaspoon baking powder
- ¼ teaspoon salt
- ½ cup milk
- 2 16-ounce cans cherry fruit filling

Melt the butter in a 1½-quart casserole. In a medium-sized bowl, sift together the flour, sugar, baking powder, and salt. Add the milk to this mixture to make a batter. Pour the cherry fruit filling into the casserole with the melted butter. Then pour the batter over the cherries and swirl into the cherries with a spatula, leaving most of the batter on top. Bake at 375° for 40 minutes. Serve warm with whipped cream or ice cream.

Pumpkin Pie

SERVES SIX

Darlene Rhodes says that this is her husband Gene's favorite pumpkin pie. These two, who call themselves the "Pumpkin People," are experts about what makes a perfect pie, so we include this recipe for your enjoyment.

- 1¾ cups cooked pumpkin or pumpkin pack from a can
- 1½ cups milk
- 3 large eggs
- 1 tablespoon molasses
- ½ teaspoon ginger
- ½ teaspoon salt
- 1 tablespoon butter or margarine, melted
- ¾ cup sugar
- 1¼ teaspoons cinnamon
- ½ teaspoon nutmeg
- 1 9-inch pie shell, unbaked

Preheat the oven to 425°. Mix all the ingredients in a large bowl and pour into the pie shell. Bake for 50 minutes. The center of the pie will be soft, but will set as the pie cools.

Authors' note: Darlene also provides a recipe for "Perfect Pie Crust," should you be inclined to make yours from scratch.

    1½ cups flour
     ½ teaspoon salt
     ½ cup butter-flavored shortening
  4-5 tablespoons cold water

Combine the flour and salt in a bowl, and cut in the shortening until it forms pea-sized chunks. Sprinkle with water, one tablespoon at a time, tossing lightly with a fork until the dough will form a ball. Wrap in waxed paper and refrigerate for 30 minutes.

With a floured rolling surface and pin, roll the dough into a circle. Trim one inch larger than an inverted nine-inch pie pan. Carefully loosen the dough from the surface with a large metal spatula and fold it into quarters. Then unfold it and press it into the pie pan, folding the edge under. Note: The less you handle the dough, the flakier it will be.

Harvest Festivals

MENTION HARVEST CELEBRATIONS TO URBAN AMERI-
cans, and they immediately think of the big, glitzy state fairs. If
they're old enough, or if they're theatre or movie buffs, they'll
imagine something like the fair in the great Rodgers and Ham-
merstein musical *State Fair*. Well, Michigan holds its great state
fair in Detroit during the first week of September, but county fairs
are smaller versions of that kind of harvest celebration, and in
Michigan they draw hundreds of thousands of annual visitors.
And that real old-time flavor of a county fair is still exciting, spiced
with the mixed smells of barns and deep-fat-fried foods from the
wagons that rim the midway.

Take a quick tour through the Allegan County Fair (held
during the second week of September) as an example. It took four
people to get it there, but the 289-pound pumpkin lies unbruised
on the cement floor at the end of the vegetable display in the
Agricultural Exhibits building. People stop, shake their heads, pat
the pumpkin, and cackle, "That's some pumpkin." Then they
wander off to inspect the latest knitting machine that will "help
you earn big dollars at home in your spare time," pass by the sets
of new and exciting no-stick pots, think about where in the farmhouse they might put one of the new, churning spas, try on one
of the baseball-style caps from the display of hundreds with a
variety of embroidered logos, listen to the demonstrators play
tunes on the pianos and electric organs, and hazard a guess on
the weight of the dressed pig in the sample freezer displayed by
the home shopping service. They could win that pig, and at worse
they'll suffer only a telephone sales call.

Emerging from the exhibits building, blinking in bright daylight, the same people stop and plunk down the fifty-cent admission charge to view the world's largest hog, or the fifteen-foot

*Allegan County
Fair*

man-eating alligator. They'll do that with good reason — everybody at the fair is interested in seeing the biggest and the best.

That's really what's important about the county fair: it's a place and time for farmers to step back from the hard work of growing things and to give and get recognition for what they've accomplished. A young farmer grew that 289-pound pumpkin, and another won the blue ribbon for those perfect McIntosh apples.

One farmer proudly hitches up his blue-ribbon team of Belgian draft horses to his freshly painted and stenciled wagon to take a drive around the barns. That lets fans admire the magnificent animals the way they were meant to be seen, not just standing in their stalls. At the other end of the barn, men and women spend an entire Saturday readying their sulkies and grooming their horses for the evening race in front of the grandstand.

That's also where the demolition derby is held, and where professional musical groups entertain in the evening. But it's also the place where high-school cheerleading squads and bands strut

Prize-winning apples shine at the Allegan County Fair.

their stuff and compete, while supporters cheer them on from the grandstand. The county fair is a world of competition, covering the whole spectrum of farm work and farm-family hobbies and activities, and kids are an important part of it all. Exhibits by 4-H members fill one hall. We listened as one proud father exclaimed his wonder over his daughter's blue ribbon for baked goods, marveling that she had done so well. She explained that baking was just one of their club's after-school projects.

Kids continuously visit and fuss with their 4-H displays, just as church women fuss over their home-decorating booths. In room-like settings with antiques and crafts, they show their baking, their home-canned tomatoes, and their preserves — all made with fruits and vegetables harvested from their own orchards and fields. These displays may all be tucked into old buildings clustered in the far corners of the fairgrounds, but they're the meaningful part of the county fairs — events that are still, above all, harvest festivals.

Michigan farmers also celebrate with the full-scale carnivals at the county fairs. Barkers shout, "Three balls! Just knock 'em down and get your choice! Get the big ones here!" High-school boys with cheerleaders on their arms step up and let fly. And sometimes they win the stuffed panda bear. Sure, the games aren't as easy as they seem, but there's always a chance to win, and it's fun to test your skills when it doesn't really matter — when it's not high-school football, when it's just fun.

And after you win the panda, it's time to strap yourself in and ride that Pirate Ship, which throws itself up in the air until you're hanging upside down, and then flings itself back the other way. It's a thrill. Or maybe you can ride the giant Ferris wheel, and from the top see the whole midway spread out beneath you. With the right partner, it's a romantic thrill, and besides, it's historic — 1993 was the centennial year of Mr. Ferris's invention.

County Festivals

The county fairs, with their honky-tonk atmosphere, greasy foods, and numerous exhibits, are fun, but Michigan offers more than just these fairs in the late summer and fall. You can enjoy specific crop festivals throughout the growing season, including ones celebrating maple syrup, strawberries, asparagus, sugar, cherries, potatoes, peaches, herbs, mint, blueberries, beans, apples, and pumpkins. And in the fall there are harvest festivals held by municipalities around the state. These smaller celebrations display all of the local pride that comes from producing something good from the land, and most feature elected royalty, games, carnivals, food booths, and parades, with every parade usually ending with the host town's fire engine, its sirens blaring. These festivals lack much of the brazenness, competitiveness, and honky-tonk atmosphere of county fairs. And somehow, these annual one-crop celebrations, run almost exclusively by local people, seem more wholesome.

Maple Syrup Festivals

It starts with maple syrup. In March, Blandford Nature Center in Grand Rapids welcomes spring with "Sugarbush." This is an annual free event that highlights the tapping of maple trees and the processing of sap into syrup. Volunteers lead tours to see the tapped trees, and you can visit the Sugarbush, where other volunteers tend the fires and evaporate the sap. Blandford's maple syrup and maple candy are available for purchase at the Sugarbush, and sales help support the center's activities.

The Cranbrook Institute of Science in Bloomfield Hills, the Chippewa Nature Center in Midland, and the Fenner Arboretum in Lansing all have maple-syrup festivals early in the spring, and the Kalamazoo Nature Center has a Maple Sugar Café.

In fact, in March you can see the aluminum pails on trees all over the state of Michigan. Whole towns with maple-lined streets — Charlevoix, for example — tap their trees and turn syrup time into community fund-raisers. And by April, the commercial farmers wind up their harvest and release the syrup to market.

For more than fifty years, the maple-syrup producers of Vermontville (between Battle Creek and Lansing) have held an annual festival on the last full weekend of April. You can join the 15,000 to 20,000 people who come to see the Saturday parade, cheer the queen who's been chosen, have a pancake breakfast (served with real maple syrup, of course), enjoy the carnival, and "dance the night away." On Sunday, there are old-fashioned games and contests, including an egg toss, arm wrestling, and wood chopping. There are also crafts and locally made maple products for sale.

Shepherd (between Alma and Mount Pleasant) has a similar maple festival on that same weekend.

Blossomtime

Also on the last weekend of April, Benton Harbor and Saint Joseph host Blossomtime. They claim this is Michigan's oldest

*Taking in the tulips — in all their lush colors and
varieties — during Tulip Time in Holland*

festival, drawing up to 250,000 visitors each year. Blossomtime
salutes the spring fruit blossoms of strawberries, blueberries,
peaches, plums, and apples. Miss Blossomtime is chosen from the
queens previously selected by the southwestern communities of
Michigan.

They are featured in the Grand Floral Parade, which has more
than a hundred floats. Each queen has her own float, and there is
a grand float for Miss Blossomtime. Blossomtime also has carnival
rides and scheduled activities that include running events, a fash-
ion show, an arts-and-crafts show, the Grand Floral Ball, and the
"Sunday Blessing of the Blossoms."

The second week in May brings Tulip Time to Holland. *Tulip Time*
Thousands of tulips are in full bloom — lining the streets, filling
the parks, and decorating planters and flower boxes in front of
every business and public building.

People from all over the country, as many as 500,000 each
year, come to enjoy Dutch food, klompen dancing, street-scrub-

bing done in the Dutch tradition, with stiff-bristled brooms, Dutch street organ music, bands, and parades. The governor often dons Dutch clothes to help scrub the streets and to lead one of the parades. Children are let out of school to participate, and all the children, regardless of ancestry, wear Dutch costumes and wooden shoes to parade and dance in the festival. They'll pose for your pictures with a smile, even if the wooden shoes hurt their feet.

Tulip Time is the best time for you to choose your bulbs for fall planting. The city of Holland presents demonstration gardens near the public library and around the authentic imported Dutch windmill in the city's Windmill Island Park. Dutch Village also labels its tulip gardens. And you can shop Veldheer's Tulip Farm for the latest varieties as well as traditional bulbs. They have acres of labeled tulips, costumed student guides, replicas of windmills and Dutch canal bridges, and observation towers to use for picture-taking. Veldheer's is a fine farm market.

National Asparagus Festival

In June in Michigan, asparagus is celebrated. The small western Michigan towns of Hart and Shelby, adjacent villages, combine to host the National Asparagus Festival during the second weekend in June. And they go all out.

Local restaurants and growers in Hart compete for trophies in a food sampling show. Asparagus soup, asparagus pickles, asparagus "guacamole," asparagus pizza, asparagus spice muffins, and asparagus stir-fry are all displayed on tables set up in a local school gym. You can taste them all and vote for your favorite. The recipe for asparagus soup included in this book was a recent winner.

In Hart, there's also an arts-and-crafts show in the park where you can buy beer-battered, deep-fried asparagus instead of French fries. Across the street from the park, Sally's Family Restaurant features asparagus omelets. Near the high school, a local ice-cream shop offers asparagus ice-cream cones for your delight. When we sampled it, the ice cream wasn't as bad as the teenager working the window warned us it would be. In fact, we liked it. It was really good vanilla ice cream with chunks of young asparagus stalks frozen in the mix. It was so cold, you couldn't taste the asparagus, but it did add crunch and color.

The big event is the Saturday parade, featuring bands, clowns, and floats, most of them decorated with asparagus. Children walk

*The Asparagus Queen and her court are the highlight
of the National Asparagus Festival.*

along with the parade, costumed as asparagus stalks, and toss
candy to their friends in the crowd. In a recent festival parade,
the Melody Mates do-si-doed on a big flatbed truck, and the
Scottville Clown Band pleased the crowd with their wonderful
big-band music and wacky costumes. The usual collection of
antique cars were scattered through the procession.

The Asparagus Queen reigns over all, and her float is the
highlight of the parade. The queen must be over eighteen, married,
and live in Oceana or an adjacent county. In 1993, the queen, who
had been nominated by her grandchildren, was seventy years old.
She was wildly cheered by the crowd.

Other festival queens — the Coast Guard Festival Queen
from Grand Haven and the Cherry Queen, for example — rode
on floats or in decorated convertibles in the parade. These ladies
were traditional pageant queens — young, shapely, and beautiful.

In the evening, an asparagus-chicken smorgasbord, a square dance, and fireworks all contribute to your enjoyment. And you can buy souvenir T-shirts, mugs, and cookbooks by local cooks who are experts with asparagus. As we left town after the celebration, wearing our new T-shirts, we were given the perfect memento: a pound of perfect, fresh-snapped asparagus.

Strawberry Festival

If you prefer strawberries, Hartford, in southwestern Michigan, celebrates these juicy Michigan berries the second weekend in June with the Strawberry Festival. The Hartford Business Association sponsors a youth parade, a "best legs" contest, a pancake breakfast, a "strawberry walk," and a "strawberry run." In Ely Park, there are arts-and-crafts booths, games and rides, the crowning of a prince and princess, and, most delicious, a pie-eating contest.

Michigan Sugar Festival

Another sweet June festival takes place in the small town of Sebewaing in the thumb of the state: the Michigan Sugar Festival, which has been celebrated annually for about thirty years. What goes on "under the beet top"? Numerous activities take place in and around this large tent, including the crowning of a prince and a princess, a children's parade, the crowning of the Sugar Queen, a circus, fireworks, live entertainment, athletic events, and barbecues. Commemorative T-shirts and other souvenirs are sold, but the sweetest memento is a free two-pound bag of Michigan sugar.

For spectators, high points of the Sugar Festival include the squaring off of the firemen and the merchants in their traditional softball game, and the firemen's staging of water battles. We talked to Kathy Manary, a captain of the ambulance service, at the city hall. She loves the festival and thinks it's fun for all, but she misses much of it herself, and bemoans the fact that she has to be on call all weekend. That's the fate of many of the volunteers as well.

Leland Wine and Food Festival

During the second week of June, Leland (in the Leelanau peninsula) holds a one-day Wine and Food Festival in its famous Fishtown district. In huge, gaily striped tents, as many as 4,000 people taste and enjoy Michigan wines and elegant food from the fine restaurants of northern Michigan's resort country. One year we counted thirteen wineries participating, and even more restaurants. And Fishtown is a small area, so all those booths and the thousands of people make the festival crowded. But it's an extremely good-humored crowd.

In a tradition that dates back to 1931, Traverse City, "The

Cherry Capital of the World," hosts the National Cherry Festival for eight days in early July. The whole Grand Traverse area gets involved with this celebration and glorification of cherries.

Many of the cherry farms in the area have tours and give you the chance to pick some of the luscious black cherries commonly grown around the city. Farm stands sell cherries, cherry preserves, and cherry butter, while larger farms like Amon's and Underwoods' sell their cherry chutney and cherry spaghetti sauce. Usually they offer tastes of new products introduced to celebrate the festival.

Downtown stores feature "cherry" items — souvenir T-shirts, posters, cookbooks, mugs, cherry-printed fabrics, and dinnerware with cherry patterns. Their windows are filled to capacity with these items and decorated with photographs of the cherry orchards and displays of the equipment used in the industry. Restaurants advertise whitefish with cherry butter, cherry pies, cherry-apple cider, cherry chicken salad, and even Hunan cherry chicken. Selkerk's, a large produce store on a corner lot on the edge of downtown, has cases of cherry Coke and wild cherry pop piled up next to an awning-covered stand where you can taste cherry-syrup–flavored drinks, ice cream, and other goodies.

Tents on the lakefront house booths with information about the festival. Here you can buy cherries, cherry products (e.g., jams, pies, and dried cherries), and certain kinds of crafts, including cherry woodworking.

The big attraction for the local young people is a four-block-long midway with carnival rides, games, and food wagons.

Three parades showcase the ingenuity of local businesses, growers, youth groups, and perhaps the entire community. The Heritage Parade primarily shows off antique cars, vintage boats, horse-drawn carts, and local bands. Five thousand children march in the Kids Parade, wearing costumes, riding decorated bikes, and taking along their pets. Any kid can participate by showing up at the proper time. The Grand Finale is the Cherry Royale Parade, which features more than twenty bands and more floats than Pasadena's Parade of Roses.

Everyone's favorite is the Williams Brothers' float, the theme of which is kept secret until the last possible moment. For years, David Williams and his brothers have planned these floats. One year their entry was titled "The Great Lakes Lumber League." At the last moment, a small rearrangement of letters revealed that it was really "The Great Lake Slumber League." Marchers wore pillows attached to their heads, identifying them as sleepwalkers, and the central float was a large bed. Each year the Williams brothers reveal the theme to the 400 people invited to participate in their entry, but only at the last moment, and it remains a surprise to the parade officials and the delighted crowds.

For the eight days of the Cherry Festival, you can eat cherries and cherry-flavored meals, build sand sculptures, enter or watch the bed race, compete in a $1,000,000 hole-in-one contest, participate in a 15K race or a mile run (this by invitation), play in a tennis tournament, or enter the cherry pie–eating contest. There's nonstop entertainment, much of it free, and fireworks (on the Fourth of July and on the final Saturday night) in the evening.

To orchestrate the 150 listed events, it takes 750 volunteers.

Two of the hundreds of volunteers who help make the National Cherry Festival a success

When asked, they say they do all that work because of local pride, and every year some 500,000 or more people enjoy the fruits of their efforts.

One event is missing at the Traverse City festival: The International Cherry Pit–Spitting Competition. For that, you'll have to go to Eau Claire in the southwest corner of the state on the first Saturday of July. The competition is put on by Tree-Mendus Fruit Farms, and the object is to break the world-record spit of 72' 7½", set there in 1988.

On the other side of the state, on the last weekend of July, the volunteer firemen of the small town of Munger, near Bay City, stage the Munger Potato Festival. For over thirty-five years, they have provided activities for families, selected the Potato Head King and Queen to lead the parade, and provided food, beer, bingo, and Vegas tents.

Munger Potato Festival

The festival features a complete carnival, craft exhibitors, an old car show, a demolition derby, a 4-H show, and polka bands. Kids compete in potato-sack races and the potato toss, or participate in potato decorating and painting. The food booths serve potato sausage, potato burgers, chicken barbecue, and "all kinds of potato treats." And literally tons of free potatoes are given away each day of the festival.

In late July or early August, it's time to head for South Haven and the National Blueberry Festival, which was first celebrated more than thirty years ago. This kicks off on a Thursday evening with the crowning of Little Miss Blueberry at the South Haven Marina. To qualify, each young lady must be seven, eight, or nine before June 30th; be a resident of the South Haven school district; and be willing to participate in the fund-raising activities, with the proceeds to be donated to the annually designated local charities. The girls' pictures are printed on voting boxes, where voters may cast their ballots by dropping in change. Residents and guests are all eligible to vote, and there's no limit to the number of times they're allowed to vote. The girl with the most money in her voting box gets to be Little Miss Blueberry. After the crowning, the world's largest blueberry pie is cut and served.

National Blueberry Festival

Good as that pie is, the messy blueberry pie–eating contest and the blueberry bubble gum–blowing contest are the favorite food events for most of the kids.

Merchants hold a sidewalk sale that lasts the four days of the festival. Things to enjoy include a carnival (try and soak a local celebrity at the dunk tank sponsored by the Optimists' Club), food tents, the Steelheaders' fish boil, and the Kiwanis' pig roast. Also featured are athletic events, a sand-sculpture contest, a tanning contest, and a "sexy legs" contest. On Saturday, fifty or more artists and crafts people show their work at the city hall. A number of them make sparkly wreaths so that every little girl can pretend to be Little Miss Blueberry.

The biggest crowds are at the Saturday parade, which features bands, floats, Miss South Haven, Miss Michigan, and the star, Little Miss Blueberry. The fire engine does bring up the rear.

We stopped to have blueberry pancakes for a late lunch, had blueberry pie at dinner, and took blueberries and blueberry muffins home for breakfast. But our favorite find was the Blueberry Fudge from Harpold's. Blue fudge looks a little suspicious, but this tasted like fresh blueberries in rich, creamy fudge.

The Michigan Blueberry Store on Phoenix Street, South Haven's main street, is run by the growers' associations, and sells fresh blueberries, T-shirts, potted blueberry plants, and blueberry-decorated china, dish towels, breadboards, stationery, and novelties.

Farms around South Haven participate by offering tours and welcoming pickers. The DeGrandchamps' farm has picnic areas, clean rest-rooms, and well-groomed bushes for easy picking. The owners offer interesting tours of their modern processing and packaging plant.

Montrose Blueberry Festival

The Montrose Blueberry Festival is also held in August near the town of Birch Run, north of Flint. The advertising for this festival promises, "You're in for a sweet treat. This fun-filled family event features activities for the entire family." Translation: there are carnival rides, a festival queen, a "super parade," and plenty of blueberries — blueberry pancakes, blueberry ice cream, blueberry pies, blueberry candy, and just plain blueberries, with a u-pick farm a short distance away.

Glad-Peach Festival

A number of small festivals, some as old and storied as the National Blueberry Festival, are also held in August. Check out the colorful Glad-Peach Festival, for example, held in and around Coloma's Baker Park on the first weekend of August. Peaches go well with blueberries, and gladiolas, perhaps Michigan's favorite flowers, go well with anything.

A favorite mid-August festival is the Saint Johns' Mint Festival, which invites you to "Come help us celebrate. . . . It grows bigger every year." Saint Johns, a small town twenty miles north of Lansing, puts on the annual festival complete with the crowning of the Mint Queen, a parade with 170 entries, professional entertainment, arts and crafts, antiques, and trips to a mint farm. Booths serve mint ice cream, mint candy, and mint beverages. And the celebration is topped off with a Peppermint Twist Dance.

In September and October, harvest festivals crowd the calendar in Michigan, with communities celebrating everything from the bean crop to the stomping of wine grapes.

On the Saturday after Labor Day, we attended "The Grape Escape" at Kalamazoo's Bronson Park. This downtown park occupies two city blocks and has spectacular floral displays, including a twenty-foot-high peacock formed out of red impatiens, and carrying a ten-foot tail of blue salvia.

For the Bronson Park celebration, run cooperatively with the celebration in nearby Paw Paw, each corner of the park has a large wine-tasting tent operated by a local service organization. In front of the large sculpture fountain (which was drained when we were there) is a stage erected for continuous entertainment, including a "celebrity grape stomp" in the evening.

Despite the adult focus that a wine celebration must have, the daytime celebration in Bronson Park is still child oriented. With a coterie of kids, costumed people roam the park, dressed as everything from Mickey Mouse to a telephone directory, with the most popular a figure dressed as a bunch of grapes. (That's a heavy costume, and the wearer requires frequent soft-drink and cigarette breaks behind a tent.)

Kids also use the playground equipment and play tag through the fountain, but they seem to spend most of their time eating. Food booths are set up both by local restaurants in cooperation with nonprofit groups and by local churches and organizations who supply and staff their own. We just loved the low-fat chicken pita sandwiches served by the Greek church.

Although we went to the festival to try new wines and foods, which we enjoyed immensely, we were also taken by the fine

*"Friars in a wine vat" is the St. Julian's entry
in the parade during "The Grape Escape."*

arts-and-crafts show set up on two adjacent streets that were closed off for the event. It's great fun to set out to buy "farm products" and wind up with art as a bonus.

Art, entertainment, food, and wine on a beautiful fall day in a beautiful city park: what more can you ask of a harvest celebration? There is more, actually, including an evening wine-sampling affair at the Kalamazoo Radisson Plaza, where, for a donation that supports an annually designated charity, you get a chance to sample more than a hundred Michigan wines, including some old and rare vintages.

But on Sunday, we shifted scenes from the sophisticated big city of Kalamazoo to the little town of Paw Paw, which is in the center of the grape-growing area and home to the St. Julian Winery and the Warner's Champagne Cellars and Bistro. This is where you can see the big parade and the annual grape-stomping competition held in a park on the shore of Maple Lake.

No little event, this grape stomp. Each swimsuit-clad team of five people climbs into a halved vat filled with grapes and stomps them, lies down and rolls on them, beats them with their hands and heads — does anything to produce a little more juice than the next team. We watched a team squish out 82½ pounds of juice in what they called the "longest two minutes of our lives," and that qualified them for the finals.

The big parade steps off on Michigan Avenue, Paw Paw's main street, and for a change, the fire engines lead off. As always, there are floats and parade units sponsored by service organizations, including the popular Shriner contingents, and a reigning queen: the Paw Paw Queen. Special parade features — Laura the Baby Elephant, for example — are popular, but the crowd favorites are, as usual, local features, including the huge grape harvester spewing out confetti and the octogenarian on a bicycle. Our favorites were the Eau Claire Cherry Festival Bag Ladies contingent and the Paw Paw Pow Wow with Books float by the Paw Paw Library.

Everywhere along the parade route, participants carry great bunches of purple balloons, looking like overgrown grapes, while other marchers wear costumes that make them look like bunches of grapes. There's no doubt what this parade celebrates.

The two wineries join the celebration with wine-tasting parties and tours. When we were there, St. Julian's opened its back room for dancing to a rock/polka ensemble, and lined the room with tasting booths. Warner's featured a keyboardist playing romantic music for diners on its deck and offered wine-tasting in its usual tasting room.

And Paw Paw, like Kalamazoo, offers much more. Arts-and-crafts booths occupy two blocks of Niles Street and some adjacent parking lots. Nearby, you can watch the champagne races, which feature teams of waiters and waitresses running an obstacle course with trays of full glasses of champagne to serve "guests" waiting at linen-covered tables at the finish line. And it's real champagne, which the winners of each heat get to drink in celebration.

And there are still other alternatives. You can spend your time leisurely taking a train ride through the vineyard country or a steamboat ride on Maple Lake. Athletes can participate in a walk, a run, or a vineyard bike tour. And for the kids, McDonald's sets up a midway of carnival rides in its parking lot.

In short, the wine festival in Kalamazoo and Paw Paw is a

major event, well choreographed and offering worlds of things to do.

On usually the same weekend, Edmore, Michigan, some sixty miles north of Grand Rapids and Lansing, presents the Michigan State Potato Festival. It's smaller than the wine festival, but big enough to offer a range of food booths (one serving potato treats only), athletic events, including a run through Deer Forest, carnival rides, an arts-and-crafts fair, a classic car show, and parades, the most unique being a Fireman's Friday Parade. Prizes are awarded for the biggest potato and the potato that most looks like a famous person. (Every year, it seems, they have multiple Mickey Mouse and Richard Nixon entries.)

Michigan State Potato Festival

At this time of year, there are so many harvest festivals that, regardless of where you live, you couldn't be more than twenty miles away from one. And apples are the king.

Starting in mid-September there's the Apple Festival in Niles, the Apple Fest in Coldwater, and an apple celebration in Mount Pleasant. In early October, there's the Belding Apple Festival, apple festivals in both Bangor and Charlevoix, and the Apple Butter Festival in Lansing. And that's not all.

Apple Festivals

In the center of an apple orchard area, Rockford, a pretty little town on the Rogue River in northern Kent County, goes all out to celebrate the harvest. On the last weekend of September and the first two weekends of October, the Rockford Harvest Festival offers free musical entertainment, craft shows and demonstrations, a horseshoe-tossing tournament, storytellers, and strolling musicians. It also features the traditional chicken barbecues, a chili challenge, and a "wienie woofer" contest. There's also an antique tractor show and a tractor pull.

Rockford Harvest Festival

The doorway of every store is decorated with pots of chrysanthemums, and every light post is adorned with bales of hay and cornstalks. And naturally, in the center of it all there's a farmers' market with homemade baked goods for sale as an extra. (Interestingly, this spectacular celebration has its roots in a homecoming celebration for Rockford High School.)

Held the same three weekends as the Rockford celebration, Kent Harvest Trails is a tour of more than twenty farms in Kent County. Bill Bos, president of the Kent Ag Tourism Council, the organization that coordinates this event, says, "Our farms really

Kent Harvest Trails

Kids are part of the parade during the Great Pumpkin Fest.

have something for everyone. It's a great way for families who have never been on a farm to enjoy a fun day together while learning about agriculture."

We've been to Le Montueux Vineyard and Winery, which offers tours, tastings, and pumpkin-picking. At Heffron Farms, we've been greeted by a purple cow who gave out balloons and invited us to take a wagon tour of a beef-cattle farm. We've watched kids make scarecrows at Orchard Hill Farm, and enjoy a "maize maze" and race zucchini-laden wheelbarrows at Country Gardens. We've watched pumpkin carving and pumpkin painting. We've had cider and doughnuts; we've picked apples at Sprik Farms (and stared at a buffalo); we've seen "Art in the Orchards" at Klackle's, selected pumpkins, and enjoyed some beautiful fall days in the country. In short, there are so many choices and places to go that the six weekend days of the Kent Harvest Trails aren't enough.

Maps of the trails are available at D & W stores, and special events like this are extensively covered in the *Grand Rapids Press* and other local papers. So take advantage of some of our perfect fall days by joining the free tours offered by these hospitable farmers in west Michigan.

Great Pumpkin Fest

The Great Pumpkin Fest in Zeeland is about the last of the real harvest festivals, although Saugatuck does hold a Halloween Harvest Festival. The Zeeland parade leads off with a fifteen-foot-tall jack-o'-lantern called the Great Pumpkin. It's big, but not as impressive as the truck burdened by the weight of the winners in the largest pumpkin contest.

Zeeland, a nice, quaint, small agricultural center which, ironically, is home to some of Michigan's most modern manufacturing industries, does the full country celebration. And everybody gets involved, including those local industries. That Great Pumpkin was built by Batts Hangers. There are scarecrow contests and find-the-pumpkin hunts sponsored by local companies. There are tractor pulls and kids' pedal-tractor pulls. Craft shows tend to feature quilting and needlework. There's a bake-off sponsored by the local D & W, foot races, and a bicycle tour.

But the big event is the parade, which features the "home-town" float competition. Our favorite was Cinderella's pumpkin coach, a float that also featured Cinderella in rags, a fairy god-mother, and kids dressed as mice. This float was followed by Prince Charming riding horseback and carrying a silver slipper. The zaniest float? It may have been a tie between Meijer's balloon model of a farmer surrounded by produce and ice-cream cones made of balloons, and the witch float sponsored by the Ottawa Republicans.

The whole town seems to march in the Saturday parade, with bands being the most prominent units. The Zeeland High School Band and the bands from the Christian high schools in the area all marched, and so did the eighth-grade band, and so did the middle-school bands. Even the Zeeland High School Alumni Band marched. There were so many people playing so much happy, festive music that spectators couldn't help but feel happy with the Great Pumpkin Fest.

By the way, the Great Pumpkin Fest, which is a three-day event, may be the only harvest festival without a queen, but there are plenty of pretty girls, including the Zeeland High School cheerleaders, who ride on top of the hook-and-ladder fire truck and end the parade.

We haven't mentioned — or attended, for that matter — all the harvest festivals in Michigan. We found most of those that we attended by stopping at highway welcome centers in the spring and picking up brochures and calendars. (Michigan operates thirteen professionally staffed centers on major highways.) We also learned that while many of the festivals we attended have been annual events for twenty years or more, new festivals are started every year, and the place, time, and facilities of existing festivals are subject to change.

One of the primary sources for information about festivals is the Michigan Travel Bureau. Write (P.O. Box 30226, Lansing, MI 48909) or call (1-800-5432-YES) for brochures and other items. The bureau publishes the useful *Travel Guide and Calendar of Events*.

Numerous convention and tourist bureaus, both local and county, can also help with information. We've found that western Michigan hosts many of the festivals, and most helpful to us as a source of information was the West Michigan Tourist Association, located at 136 E. Fulton Street, Grand Rapids, MI 49503 (ph. [616] 456-8557). This association publishes an annual travel guide with an extensive calendar of events, and also serves as a repository for brochures produced by member firms and organizations.

Books We Think You'll Enjoy

Books specifically about Michigan

Freedman, Eric. *Michigan Free*. Ann Arbor, Mich.: University of Michigan Press, 1993.

This book basically describes a variety of wineries, cider mills, and festivals that charge no admission fee. It is a useful travel-and-recreation guide, made more useful by its inclusion of a list of the addresses and phone numbers of many local chambers of commerce.

Guthrie, Margaret. *Best Recipes of Michigan Inns and Restaurants*. Amherst, Wis.: Amherst Press, 1987.

This is a collection of recipes from Guthrie's favorite Michigan chefs.

House, Deanna. *House Specialties*. Ada, Mich.: House Specialties, 1983.

————. *More House Specialties*. Ada, Mich.: House Specialties, 1986.

————. *Even More House Specialties*. Ada, Mich.: House Specialties, 1992.

These three cookbooks by a Grand Rapids home economist and food columnist include produce recipes for both the conventional oven and the microwave.

Hunt, Don, and Mary Hunt. *Michigan Fresh*. Albion, Mich.: Midwestern Guides, 1992.

The Hunts provide an annotated, extensive listing of u-pick farms, farmers' markets, cider mills, and bakeries.

Main, Gayle. *Michigan: Savor Its Flavors*. Okemos, Mich.: Mainly Food, 1991.

This slim book, illustrated with great photographs of elegantly presented dishes, features recipes using Michigan-grown fruits and vegetables.

A Taste of Michigan. Lansing, Mich.: Michigan Restaurant Association, 1992.

As the publication information suggests, this comb-bound collection contains recipes from restaurants that belong to the Michigan Restaurant Association. You may order this book directly from the association. The phone number is (517) 482-5244.

Woody, Laurie. *Good Food from Michigan*. Three Rivers, Mich.: River Run Press, 1991.

Laurie Woody suggests methods to select, store, and prepare twenty-four Michigan-grown fruits and vegetables.

Cookbooks using farm-fresh produce

Adams, Marcia. *Heartland: The Best of the Old and New from Midwest Kitchens*. New York: Clarkson N. Potter, 1991.

This beautifully illustrated book has recipes from restaurants and cooks from Michigan and seven other midwestern states.

Branch, Susan. *Vineyard Seasons*. Boston: Little, Brown, 1988.

Susan Branch, a talented graphic artist as well as cook, hand-lettered and illustrated with watercolors this pretty collection of seasonal recipes.

Farmer's Market Cookbook. Des Moines: Better Homes and Gardens, 1993.

A fruit-and-vegetable-only cookbook, this has lots of recipes, some tips on buying and storing, and nice photos.

Loomis, Susan Hermann. *Farmhouse Cookbook*. New York: Workman, 1991.

The author traveled 20,000 miles collecting farm recipes, and they're good, even if she did miss Michigan.

Meyers, Paula. *The Art of Seasonal Cooking*. New York: Simon & Schuster, 1991.

These through-the-year recipes use only in-season produce, when things have reached their peak.

Olney, Judith. *Judith Olney's Farm Market Book*. New York: Doubleday, 1991.

This nicely illustrated coffee-table book presents recipes that require fresh produce. Olney includes fascinating interviews with famous big-city chefs who talk about the extraordinary measures they must take to buy the freshest of the fresh.

Rosso, Julee. *Great Good Food*. New York: Crown, 1993.

In her latest book, this Saugatuck innkeeper and well-known cookbook author features lower-fat cooking for "five seasons." Most of her recipes use fresh ingredients from the garden.

Shultz, Philip Stephen. *Celebrating America Cookbook*. New York: Simon & Schuster, 1994.

This book offers twelve months of feasting, highlighting holidays and festivals (including Traverse City's National Cherry Festival).

Smith, Bea. *Four Seasons Cookbook*. Marquette, Mich.: Avery Color Studios, 1993.

Smith, a Traverse City author, starts with maple-syrup recipes and follows with other seasonal preparations. The book features special holiday dishes.

Wilson, Lynne C. *Wilson Farm Country Cookbook*. Reading, Mass.: Addison Wesley, 1985.

These wonderful recipes come from Lexington, Massachusetts, and from our daughter's favorite farm stand. We love to go with her to this 100-year-old farm, regardless of the season. The owners always manage to have magnificent displays of local produce.

Wyler, Susan. *Cooking from a Country Farmhouse*. New York: Harper/Collins, 1993.

A former New York City food editor at Food & Wine *moves to northeastern Pennsylvania and becomes a garden and country cook. Some of the recipes are from her neighbors, and most are low-fat, healthy dishes using garden produce.*

Index

You can order additional copies of this book

BY PHONE: call (toll free) with credit card orders only

800-253-7521

BY FAX: fax completed order form with credit-card information to

616-459-6540

BY MAIL: send completed order form with payment to

Order Department
Wm. B. Eerdmans Publishing Co.
255 Jefferson Ave. S.E.
Grand Rapids, MI 49503

Please send me _____ copies of *Celebrate the Harvests!*
(ISBN 0-8028-7056-2)
at **$14.99 each** (shipping included)

Total amount $ _____

_____ payment enclosed
_____ please charge my credit card:

☐ Visa   ☐ MC   ☐ American Express   ☐ Discover

Card # _____   Expiration Date: _____

Signature _____

Name _____

Address _____

City _____ State _____ ZIP _____

Phone (_____) _____